NORTH STAR
TO FREEDOM

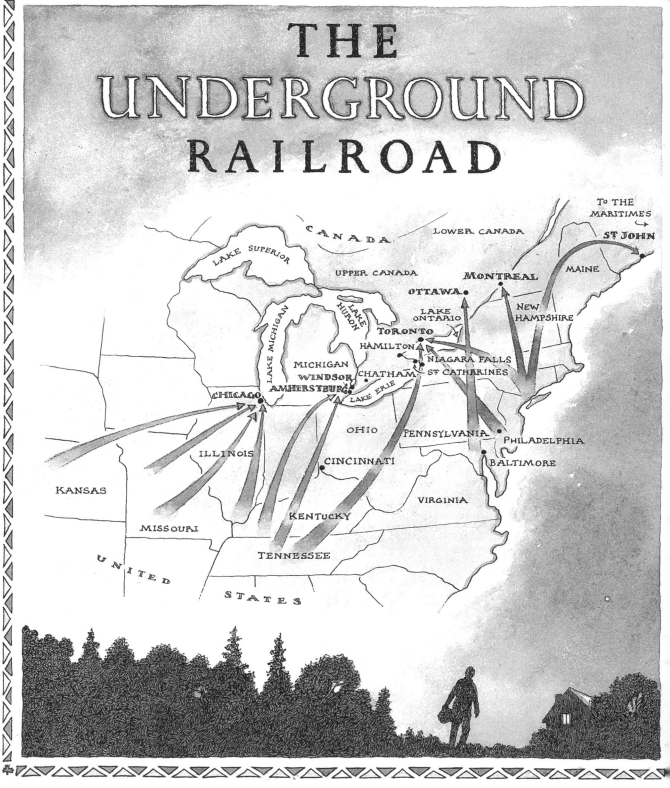

NORTH STAR
TO FREEDOM

THE STO DETROIT PUBLIC LIBRARY AILROAD

Published by
Delacorte Press
an imprint of Random House Children's Books
a division of Random House, Inc.
1540 Broadway
New York, New York 10036

Text copyright © 1996 by Gena K. Gorrell
Typesetting and design by MacTrix DTP
Map by Malcolm Cullen

First American Edition 1997 published by Delacorte Press
Originally published in Canada in 1996 by Stoddart Publishing Company Ltd., Ontario

Visit us on the Web! www.randomhouse.com/kids

Educators and librarians, for a variety of teaching tools, visit us at www.randomhouse.com/teachers

ISBN: 0-385-32607-6

RL: 4.6

Reprinted by arrangement with Delacorte Press

Printed in the United States of America

January 2000

10 9 8 7 6 5 4 3 2 1

To all those whose names have been forgotten

Contents

Publisher's Note

◆⇥══◉ ◉══⇤◆

In the period of history covered in this book, the geographical names in North America changed often. We have tried to use terms that clearly identify the area being discussed, without necessarily noting every official change in name.

The terms for North Americans of African (or partially African) descent have similarly changed. "People of color" is too general and rather cumbersome, and sounds obtrusively modern for this historical book. "African Americans" is ambiguous in a context that includes African Canadians. We have therefore settled on the term "black" as being concise, specific, and (we hope) unobtrusive. Terms within quotations have been left unchanged, as they reflect the reality of the past.

There are many accounts of slavery in the New World, and how it was first resisted and later abolished, but these accounts often do not agree. Many slaves were illiterate, and depended on others to tell their stories. Given the strong feelings on both sides, no doubt both the abolitionists and the supporters of slavery found it convenient, at times, to "improve" the facts. Where the historical data are unclear, we have tried to speak generally; whatever the exact dates and numbers, the human essence of this epic struggle remains the same.

Foreword

⊰⚌⊙⚌⊱

In the Jamaica of my youth, we studied history. We learned about the shifting and changing of the great European nations. We read about wars and betrayals and intrigues and complicated misunderstandings that resulted in empires rising and falling. We knew the stories of kings and queens. It was heady stuff.

Oh, we knew that we had come to Jamaica as slaves. But our history books often focused on the great abolitionists who had worked to end the traffic in human lives, and to free our ancestors to live as full participating British subjects enjoying all of the benefits that entailed. It was many years later, when I was almost into adulthood, that I learned the full history of the slave trade—what it did, what it meant to my ancestors, what it means to black people in North America today. Such knowledge changed my life. I found that we had not been passive in this great drama. I learned about heroes, some whose names we knew. I also learned about the hundreds of nameless men, women, and children who broke their own chains.

North Star to Freedom is a very important book because it helps us understand one of the most shameful episodes in our history. Equally important, it tells about the humane, courageous, and decent acts of people, black and white, in the face of that travesty.

This is a book that has been a long time coming. Gena Gorrell's telling of the story is accurate. The pain and the suffering are there, but the bitterness is not, for it is a story full of hope. Unfortunately, it is a story that is not yet over.

It would be comfortable to assume that slavery, a practice that blighted millions of lives for thousands of years in cultures in different parts of the world, has disappeared. It has not. There are still many places where people, including children younger than those reading this book, are economic or political slaves.

The Underground Railroad, constructed of dry riverbeds, leafy country lanes, quiet farms, bustling city streets, and most of all, human courage, remains a symbol of the very worst and very best in human beings. It is a glowing example of what ordinary people can do to right a terrible wrong. Gena Gorrell writes, "While the story of slavery is an ugly one, it is finally a story of justice overcoming injustice. It is a story of wrongs being made right." The quest for freedom is not over. The story of the Underground Railroad allows us to honor those who came before it, while it inspires us to address injustices in our own troubled times.

— Rosemary Brown

Introduction

⋆⇀═◎ ═⇀⋆

It's the middle of the night, and you're suddenly wide awake. What was that noise?

"Hush . . . don't wake the others! Just lie still and don't make a sound!"

It's your mother—but what's she doing at this hour? The sky is black, and you can see stars through the cracks in the shed roof. The boards beneath you are hard, and a splinter is digging into your back, but you try not to move. As the cold night wind blows through the walls, you pull your thin jacket closer around you. You can hear Uncle Frank's deep breathing, and Auntie is snoring a little.

"Get up and slip out the door. Don't take anything—just creep out quiet as a mouse!"

As you tiptoe through the half-open door, she's right behind you, carrying a bundle. She takes your hand and hurries you down the cattlepath. It's hard to walk in the dark with bare feet; you can't see where the stones are, and you stub your toes.

"Are we going to Papa?"

"No. Papa's gone, child, I told you that. They sent him away and I got no idea where to find him." Even in her whisper, you can hear her voice tremble.

"Then where are we going?"

"Not so loud! We're going to Canada."

"Where's Can — "

"Don't ask me where it is, or how far! All I know is, we walk toward the North Star and pray God will take care of us. All I know is, we can't stay here no more! They took away your papa, they took away your brother, and I'm not waiting till they take you too!"

She's walking so fast that it's hard to keep up with her, but at least you don't feel cold anymore. You're just trying to sort things out in your mind when she speaks again, this time more calmly, but so seriously that your stomach turns right over.

"We're going together, child, and I pray the good Lord will get us both to Canada. But if anything happens to me, don't you stop — just keep follow- ing that star. Because beginning tonight — beginning the minute we walked out of that shed back there — we're free. And we're not ever going to be slaves again."

"Free" is a word we hear often in the modern world. People speak of being free to say what they think, free to read what they like, free to go where they want and do what they want.

In most modern countries, people's freedoms are protected by law, and they're often taken for granted. It's easy to forget that throughout history, many people have lived their whole lives as slaves, with little or no personal freedom. Even in the United States and Canada, slavery was a fact of life just a few generations ago.

After European explorers "discovered" the Americas about five hundred years ago, the Europeans needed workers to exploit the riches of the "New World." In the next few centuries, many thousands of black people were captured in Africa and brought to North America as slaves. A few made daring escapes, but most were trapped in a captivity of hard labor and cruel treatment.

As time went by, slavery became illegal in the northern part of the United States and in Canada. More and more slaves dared to run away from the southern states, although they knew they would be punished terribly if they were caught. They headed north, traveling at night so that they wouldn't be seen, and using the North Star to guide them.

Some slaves made the dangerous trip with no assistance except an occasional scrap of food or word of advice from someone they happened to meet along the way. But others were helped by a secret network of people, both black and white, who together helped runaways find their way to freedom. The secret network was known as the Underground Railroad. This is the story of how it worked, and of some of the people who took part in it.

A History Written in Tears

You rise before dawn. No need to dress—you've slept in your clothes to keep warm. But your bare feet are cold, and your cheek still hurts where the young master punched you yesterday. Why did he do that? It wasn't your fault his puppy nipped him. Still, better be extra careful today.

Out in the yard, you start pumping water into buckets. Last year you could hardly work the pump's stiff handle; now it's your job to carry water into all the bedrooms before the family wake up. And quietly, or you'll be in trouble again.

As you fill the buckets you think only of your weary arms, and your empty stomach, and the throb of your cheek. But later, after you've filled the young master's washbasin, you stop to look at the drowsing hump of his body in the soft bedding, the toys and games around him, the bright-eyed puppy watching you from the bed. And you wonder yet again: why does he get so much? Why is he the lucky one? Why do you have to be the slave?

(opposite) This sculpture of slaves is from an Egyptian tomb. In ancient days, when people had more children than they could afford to feed, they sometimes sold a few of them into slavery, to get money to feed the rest. If the children were lucky enough to become household slaves in a rich home, they might live quite comfortable lives. Just a hundred years ago, children of poor families would become servants for much the same reason: the work was hard and the pay was almost nothing, but at least they would "get their knees under a good table" — in other words, go to sleep with a full stomach every night.

There have been slaves through most of human history. Their lives varied from place to place and time to time, but in general a slave was someone who was "owned" by somebody else. Slaves often had no rights as human beings. They were bought and sold as if they were pieces of furniture.

Slaves could be forced to do any kind of work, without pay. If they refused to work, they could be beaten or starved. They had to live where they were told to live, and they ate whatever food their owners gave them. They could even be taken away from their families and sold to other owners; they might never see their loved ones again.

SLAVES OF THE STATE

In early history, often people became slaves when their nation lost a war. Since there was hardly any machinery in those days, national projects like building temples and pyramids, or digging silver and gold mines, took a great deal of physical labor—labor that was not only hard but dangerous. Instead of making their own people do this work, some rulers captured thousands of men, women, and children from neighboring lands, and used them as slaves. Many slaves died on these projects, from accidents or cruel treatment.

HOUSEHOLD SLAVES

As ancient empires like those of Greece and Rome expanded, seizing control of one land after another, many of the conquered people were sold in slave markets. A Greek historian named Strabo claimed that one market alone—on the Greek island of Delos—could sell ten thousand slaves a day. Slaves were bought by private citizens, as unpaid farm laborers or household servants. In an age before washing machines, sewing machines, or vacuum cleaners, domestic chores took many hours

Victorious Roman soldiers took their defeated enemies as prisoners, to be sold into slavery. In the Roman Empire, slaves who were good fighters were trained as "gladiators" and sent into the arena to fight each other — or sometimes wild animals — to the death, to amuse spectators. In 73 B.C. a slave named Spartacus escaped from gladiators' school and led a revolt of forty thousand slaves. For two years the rebels moved through Italy, defeating Roman armies, but then Spartacus died in battle. Six thousand of his followers were caught and crucified as a warning to other rebellious slaves.

of hand labor—an early Greek writer described the slave's life as one of "work, punishment, and food." Having a houseful of slaves to serve the family's every wish was not only convenient but also proof of how important and fashionable the family was.

Although these farm and household slaves were used as free labor and had little liberty, most of them were not cruelly treated. After all, they weren't that different from the people who owned them. Many came from nearby lands and looked much like their owners. They might have similar backgrounds and be used to the same style of life. Slaves were

Captives on the long march to Egypt, locked in heavy wooden restraints to keep them from escaping.

Merchants quibble over the price of black slaves in the slave market of Baghdad (now the capital of Iraq).

sometimes set free by their owners, or managed to save enough money to "buy themselves" and become free. On the other hand, free citizens could be put into slavery for owing a lot of money or committing crimes. Sometimes owners married their slaves. One way or another, the line between slaves and owners was often crossed—so slaves were usually recognized as human beings like their owners, only less fortunate.

After the end of the Roman Empire and the spread of Christianity, slavery became less common in Europe, and by the Middle Ages it had been replaced by other forms of labor. But slavery continued to flourish in the Arab countries and other places, and many of the slaves were black people brought from Africa. They were captured in their native lands and marched along endless caravan routes across the deserts, or sailed down the muddy waters of the Nile River. Then they were sold off in the slave markets for all kinds of work, from growing dates and coffee in desert oases to diving for pearls in the Red Sea.

EUROPE DISCOVERS A "NEW WORLD"

Slaves were not the only "merchandise" traveling by caravan. Most of the goods traded between Europe and the East were sent by that slow and perilous route. Valuables like silks, spices, glassware, precious metals, and gems were sent across the known world by horse and by camel. Sometimes they never arrived; whole caravans could be buried by sand-storms, or snatched by bandits.

But in the 1400s a Portuguese prince known as Henry the Navigator began a new age of exploration. Henry founded a school of navigation (sailing) and geography, and sent navigators out to look for faster, safer trade routes over the ocean. His ships made their way to Africa and came back triumphantly with rich cargoes of gold and slaves. By the time Henry died in 1460, seven or eight hundred slaves were being transported to Portugal annually, and soon the most daring sea captains of Europe were competing to find shortcuts to the wealth of China

When Europeans arrived in South America, they brutally enslaved the local people. But slavery was not new to the Americas. The Aztecs of Central America enslaved their defeated enemies, and sometimes fattened them up to be sacrificed. The native peoples of Canada's Northwest Coast used their enemies as household slaves.

and India. They were sailing west across the ocean, in the hope of finding the Far East.

What they found instead, of course, was the "New World"—what we now call North America, Central America, and South America.

NEW WORLD SLAVERY

When the Europeans began meeting the native inhabitants of these strange lands that blocked their path to the East, they learned that some of them had wonderful gold ornaments and treasures. The rumor spread that the New World had vast gold deposits, and the nations of Europe— mainly Britain, France, Holland, Portugal, and Spain—began a fierce rivalry for these lands and their supposed treasures.

They also began the backbreaking work of building cities, digging mines, and clearing farmland. At first they tried enslaving the local people to do the labor, but this plan didn't work very well. Many of the natives had fled or been killed during the invasion, or had died of diseases they caught from the Europeans. The survivors were on familiar ground, and many were able to escape or rebel. With so much work to be done, who was going to do it?

The answer was a brutal and heartless one that would change the face of the New World forever.

The Europeans decided to import masses of slaves—tens of thousands, and eventually millions—all the way from Africa. The Africans would find it difficult to run away in this distant and unfamiliar land—and if they did manage to escape, their dark skins would mark them as fugitives. They would be slaves for life, and their children would be slaves after them.

The Dreadful Passage

⊷⭢⟹ ⟸⭠⊷

They snatched you from your village and clamped iron chains and shackles on you, and marched you till your feet were raw and bleeding. Now you see the ocean for the first time, as they drive you onto a wooden ship that rolls and tosses in the waves. Around you, other captives weep in grief and terror. You stumble up the ramp, and a rough hand shoves you through a hole in the deck, so that you land on the people in the dark below. The ship has made many voyages, and the stink of human misery makes you gag. There's no room to stand up and no room to sit down, yet they cram in more and more people. Where are they taking you? Why are they doing this to you?

The first slave ships arrived in the New World from Africa in the early 1500s, landing their human cargo in the mainly Spanish and Portuguese colonies of South America and Central America. A hundred years later, the slave trade expanded to North America, to supply the British and French colonies of New England and New France.

(opposite) When captives of more than one slave trader were loaded onto the same ship, the traders' marks of ownership were sometimes burned into the slaves' skin with hot irons — as cattle are branded today. You can see the ship in the background, about to be loaded for the long trip across the Atlantic.

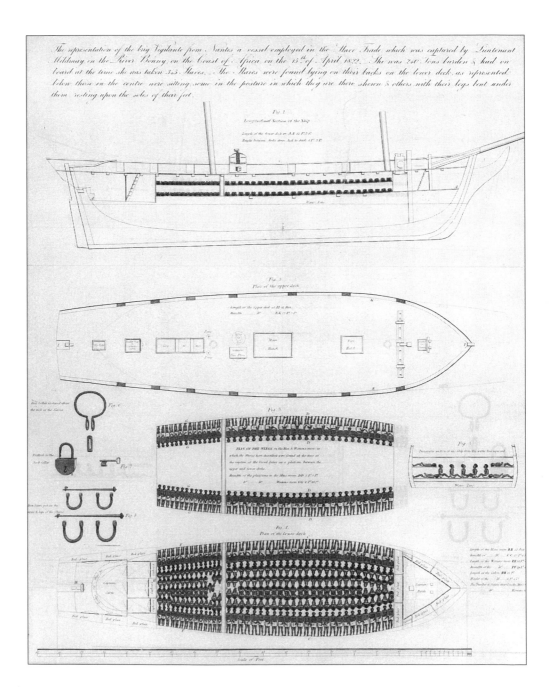

WHERE DID THE SLAVES COME FROM?

Some of the people sold into slavery had been ambushed and captured by slave traders—merchants, mostly European or Arab, who bought and sold people as a product. Others had been caught by fellow Africans.

Why would the Africans sell each other into slavery? There were fierce rivalries between some of the African peoples, and it was not uncommon for one tribe to have slaves from another tribe. Slave traders would offer rewards—including cloth, gin and rum, guns and gunpowder, and iron and copper to make tools—in exchange for slaves from an enemy tribe. Then the second tribe would have to join in the slave trade as well, to avenge the loss of their relatives, and to get guns to protect themselves against further raids. And so the Africans were cornered into preying upon each other, devastating their own people, while the slave traders sat back and grew comfortably rich.

The stories of capture are heartrending. Sometimes a whole village would be attacked, everyone who resisted would be murdered, and then the others—many of them children—would be marched away. Other

---

(opposite) This plan of a slave ship shows how tightly the captives were packed. On the lower left, some of the iron instruments used to shackle them are depicted. On the lower right, the slaves' positioning is illustrated: those in the middle could only sit up, while those on the sides could only lie down. To the captains of these ships, the men, women, and children they carried were just another cargo — to be packed as tightly as possible, and delivered with the least possible expense. Some felt it was more profitable to keep their captives alive by taking slightly better care of them; others simply packed the hold as solidly as they could, and tossed overboard the bodies of those who died.

---

times, a few victims, preferably young children, would be hastily kidnapped when no one was looking. This happened to a young Ibo boy named Olaudah Equiano:

> Owi was my younger sister, a year younger than I, and we were always together. . . . On this particular day we were sitting together on the hot sand and drawing pictures in the space between our knees. Then, so quick and horrible, we were dragged apart by heavy red hands. My mouth wrapped tight, I was stuffed into a sack. The same thing was happening to Owi. . . .

When Olaudah's parents came home from working the fields, both children were gone. Olaudah survived to become a slave and later a freeman in America, and to tell his story. We don't know what happened to his sister.

THE JOURNEY OF MISERY

Once they'd been captured, people were chained and shackled and marched to the coast in a procession called a "coffle." Anyone who resisted or was too weak to keep up was whipped. Some people died along the way, from the beatings, or from grief, illness, and exhaustion. Those who survived the march to the coast were penned up on shore until a ship came to carry them away. If the ship was delayed, they might all die before it arrived.

Austin Bearse, a sailor who sometimes worked on slave ships, described how slaves were treated:

They were separated from their families and connections with as little concern as calves and pigs are selected out of a lot of domestic animals. . . . We used to allow the relatives and friends of the slaves to come on board and stay all night with their friends, before the vessel sailed. In the morning it used to be my business to pull off the hatches and warn them that it was time to separate, and the shrieks and cries at these times were enough to make anyone's heart ache. . . .

During the crossing, the slaves were sometimes brought up on deck and forced to exercise so that they would live long enough to be sold. If they refused, they would be whipped.

Many of the captives had never seen the ocean before, and they were terrified at the sight. They were dragged out on the beaches, and sometimes stripped naked for the trip—for cleanliness, the traders said. Then, still weeping for their lost families, still sick and injured, they were packed onto sailing ships for a voyage that might last six weeks or more.

The men were usually chained together or put into leg-irons, and crammed as tightly into the hold as the captain dared. Often there was so little headroom that they could not sit upright. Women and children might be locked below, or let out on deck. The ships were desperately overcrowded and unhealthy, with little fresh air, no toilets, and scant water and food. Diseases like smallpox and dysentery spread rapidly, and many people died. Some captives took their own lives, by hanging or starving themselves, or finding a chance to throw themselves overboard. All in all, millions of the people captured in Africa for the slave trade never lived to see their destination.

Despite the terrible conditions, a few captives still managed to escape. In 1839, some fifty Africans aboard the Spanish slave ship *Amistad* (the name means "friendship") staged a revolt under their leader, Joseph Cinque; killed the captain and three sailors; and ordered the rest of the crew to sail back to Africa. The sailors tricked them and sailed to the United States instead, but in 1841—after a desperate legal battle that

(opposite) Ninety-four Africans survived this voyage of the Dembia; *many others probably died along the way. No one knows how many millions of people were caught in the slave trade, but a large percentage of them never even reached the New World.*

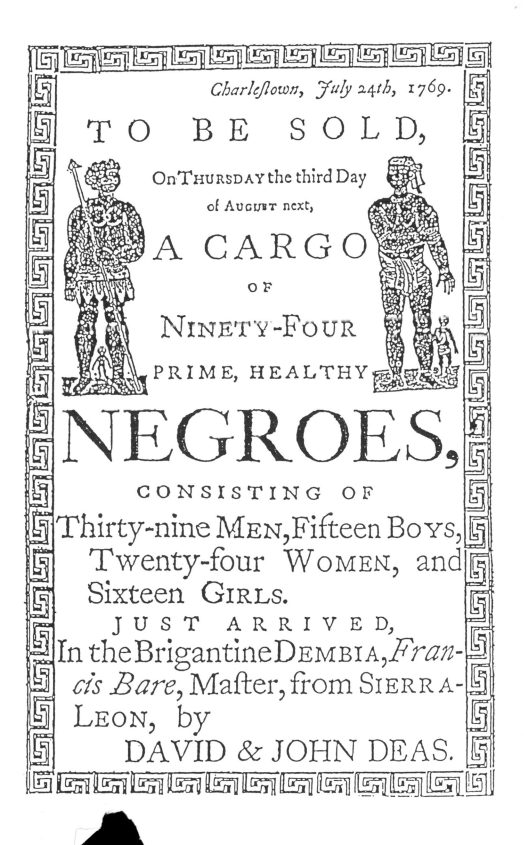

Charlestown, *July* 24th, 1769.

TO BE SOLD,

On THURSDAY the third Day
of AUGUST next,

A CARGO

OF

NINETY-FOUR

PRIME, HEALTHY

NEGROES,

CONSISTING OF

Thirty-nine MEN, Fifteen BOYS,
Twenty-four WOMEN, and
Sixteen GIRLS.

JUST ARRIVED,

In the Brigantine DEMBIA, *Francis Bare*, Master, from SIERRA-LEON, by

DAVID & JOHN DEAS.

went all the way to the U.S. Supreme Court—the Africans were freed and allowed to go home.

THE COLONIAL SLAVE MARKET

When the slave ships arrived in the harbors of the New World, the surviving slaves were herded out of the dark, stinking holds. Those who were too thin were fattened up for a few days, and those who were obviously diseased or injured might have their sores and scars covered up with paint. Gray hairs were plucked out, or covered with blacking, to make slaves look younger. Then the slaves were forced to sing and dance, and pretend to be happy, as they were put up for sale. Fashionable ladies and gentlemen of the colonies closely inspected those on offer, looking for healthy, strong bodies; quibbled over prices; and then took their new purchases home. Families were split up without pity—husbands and wives, parents and children, were sold off to different families. Even the Africans' names were lost, as they were renamed to suit their new "owners." From now on they would not be real people, but possessions.

(opposite) When the ship arrived in the New World, the most valuable slaves were sold at highly competitive public auctions. Those who looked weak or likely to die were sold more hastily, by "candle auction" — buyers could bid only for the length of time it took a candle to burn down one inch. When there were too many slaves on the market, buyers could find bargains in a "scramble sale" — they paid a flat rate for the right to rush onto the ship and snatch up whatever slaves caught their eye.

Building a World on Slavery

⊷⊐◉ ◉⊏⊷

This is a terrible country! It's cold even when the sun shines, so people hide in their gloomy shacks as much as they can. The clothes are tight and scratchy, and the food is dry and funny-tasting. You can't go out and pick something to eat, because all the plants are different here, and you can't tell what's poison. The white people want you to do all kinds of stupid things, and they get angry because you can't understand them when they talk. The other Africans try to be kind, but they're not from your tribe and they can't speak your language either.

This morning you all had to go to another house, with a big bell ringing on the roof, and sit there while white people shouted and sang (what strange singing!) under a statue of a thin white man hanging on a kind of cross. They acted as if he was some kind of god, but you thought he looked dead. Where are your own gods? Are they dead too? Is there nobody to help you?

The difference between the slaves and the slave owners—in looks, in customs, in experience—was the foundation of perhaps the cruelest and longest-lasting aspect of New World slavery. Unlike so many slave owners of earlier times, the colonials were not forced to accept the Africans as people like themselves, people who had been driven into temporary slavery by misfortune. They were able to look at them and say,

The huge plantations of the southern American colonies provided a wealthy and elegant lifestyle for plantation owners and their families — but only because slaves supplied cheap labor. Usually the teams of black laborers were supervised and punished by black "overseers," who were supervised and punished, in turn, by white overseers.

The master of a Brazilian sugar plantation punishes his slaves while his family watches. Slave labor was used to grow a huge sugar crop in South America and the islands of the Caribbean, for export and for rum-making. Because the slaves far outnumbered the whites, the owners used brutal measures to keep them in submission. The governor of the French West Indies explained in 1767, "The safety of the whites demands that the negroes should be kept in the most profound ignorance." Where exhaustion and ignorance were not enough, some owners used whippings, torture by fire, and mutilation.

"They're not like us. They don't look like us or act like us. They don't seem to think the way we think, so they obviously don't feel the way we feel. *Their race must not be as good as ours.*"

And how convenient this belief was! For if the Africans were so different, that was an excuse for their lives to be different too. They could be fed scraps, like animals; housed in shacks, like animals; worked under the whip, like animals. Some owners even declared that blacks had no souls. Of course, slave owners were not all the same: there were brutal people who whipped and overworked and underfed their slaves till they died, and there were kind people who treated their slaves with consideration and worried about their welfare. Ultimately, though, slavery in North America was based on the assumption that blacks were something less than real people.

But although most slave owners thought they were naturally "superior" to their slaves, they worried constantly about keeping them "in their place." Household slaves sometimes had close, affectionate relationships with the families who owned them, but outdoor slaves were often treated with suspicion and contempt. They were expected to be humble to their masters, and not even look them directly in the eye. In some states they couldn't leave the property without written permission, and they could be stopped and searched at any time, at any place. They were usually forbidden to meet together, for fear they would plot rebellion. They were often denied musical instruments, because they might use them to send messages. Those who challenged the system — by being defiant or simply "uppity" — were severely punished.

Most owners were especially careful to see that their slaves

When slaves were put up for auction — even if they were being sold away from their families — they were ordered to put on a good show, to fetch the best possible price for their owner. An ex-slave named John Brown explained,

When spoken to, they must reply quickly, with a smile on their lips, though agony is in their heart, and the fear trembling in their eye. They must answer every question, and do as they are bid, to show themselves off; dance, jump, walk, leap, squat, tumble, and twist about, that the buyer may see they have no stiff joints, or other physical defect.

never learned to read and write. After all, people who read books and newspapers might come across all sorts of dangerous ideas — ideas about freedom and equality. Besides, people who could read and write could communicate across distances, and perhaps plan to revolt.

So, while many owners insisted that their slaves depended on them and weren't capable of managing their own lives, in truth they were terrified that the slaves might rebel. They realized — though they might not admit it — that if the slaves were given any chance at all, the whole system of slavery might fall apart — and with it, their own way of life. Even Frederick Douglass, an ex-slave who became a leader in the fight against slavery, noted that the system could not survive without cruelty:

> Beat and cuff your slave, keep him hungry and spiritless, and he will follow the chain of his master like a dog; but feed and clothe him well — work him moderately — surround him with physical comfort — and dreams of freedom intrude.

RESISTANCE AND REBELLION

Why did the blacks put up with the poverty and injustice inflicted on them? Many didn't. Some resisted in small ways, by working slowly, or pretending to be sick, or deliberately doing things wrong. Some learned the precious skill of reading, and secretly passed it on. Slaves were often accused of stealing, but with no money and no property, they had to take whatever they could get. Josiah Henson, a slave who escaped to Canada, remembered how his friends and family had been kept starving:

but my master had plenty of sheep and pigs, and sometimes I have picked out the best one I could find . . . , carried it a mile or two into the woods, slaughtered it, cut it up, and distributed it among the poor creatures, to whom it was at once food, luxury, and medicine. Was this wrong?

Some slaves rebelled openly against their owners, and were flogged or killed as punishment. In 1739, for example, a rebellion in South Carolina led to the deaths of more than forty blacks and about thirty whites. The very next year saw another rebellion, involving as many as two hundred blacks, and this time fifty of them were hanged on the gallows as punishment. With each rebellion the slave owners felt more threatened, and the laws oppressing blacks became more and more severe.

Rather than turn to violence, many slaves tried to escape and run away. But where could they hide? Where would their dark skins not mark them as escaped "property"? In some places they weren't allowed out after dark without a lighted lantern, so any black traveling secretly was automatically guilty—and a slave caught too far from home could be executed if just two witnesses said he or she had been running away. A few blacks did make their way to small islands off the Atlantic coast, where they formed new societies based partly on their African traditions. Others found refuge with the native peoples—the Seminole Indians of Florida, in particular, gave shelter to runaways and sometimes intermarried with them. Still others fled and took new names, and hid among free blacks: one fugitive, Crispus Attucks, fled his Massachusetts owner in 1750 and hid for almost

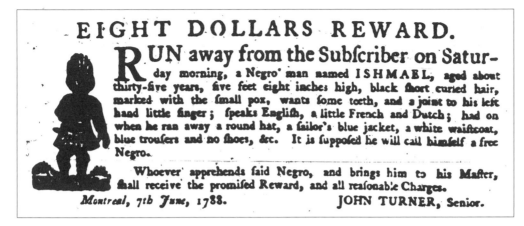

EIGHT DOLLARS REWARD.

RUN away from the Subscriber on Saturday morning, a Negro man named ISHMAEL, aged about thirty-five years, five feet eight inches high, black short curled hair, marked with the small pox, wants some teeth, and a joint to his left hand little finger; speaks English, a little French and Dutch; had on when he ran away a round hat, a sailor's blue jacket, a white waistcoat, blue trousers and no shoes, &c. It is supposed he will call himself a free Negro.

Whoever apprehends said Negro, and brings him to his Master, shall receive the promised Reward, and all reasonable Charges.

Montreal, 7th June, 1788.　　　　JOHN TURNER, Senior.

Many slaves escaped from their masters, but where could they go from there? Their very color marked them as probable runaways, and newspaper notices would promise generous rewards for their return.

twenty years, probably by working among the free blacks on trading and whaling ships.

For not all the blacks in the colonies were slaves. There were some who had freely migrated to New England or New France to seek their fortune. Others had been slaves, but had acquired enough money to buy their freedom; still others had been freed as a reward for good service (a few owners wrote it into their wills that their slaves should be freed when the owners died). When whites defied convention and had children with their slaves, the mixed-race children were sometimes free.

THE PLANTATION SOUTH AND THE INDUSTRIAL NORTH
In the more southern parts of British North America—in what is now Virginia, Maryland, Georgia, and North and South Carolina—the

Although slaves were seen as inferior, those who worked as personal servants were sometimes loved and trusted like members of the family. But if the family had money troubles, they might still be sold off to strangers.

economy was based on crops like coffee, sugar, rice, and tobacco. Much of this produce was grown on vast farms called "plantations," which needed an immense amount of cheap labor. The first Africans reached Virginia in 1619, but by the end of the 1600s thousands were arriving in the New World every year. As the slave population grew, the great plantations became richer and richer—and the owners had more and more political and economic influence. Many built splendid mansions, and copied the elegant fashions of the aristocrats of Europe. But their leisure and wealth were built on the labor of their slaves.

On the other hand, while slavery existed in the more northern colonies—in what is now Vermont, Massachusetts, Rhode Island, Pennsylvania, and New York—it was not as important to the economy. The long winters made for a short growing season, so the north had to depend more on manufacturing and other businesses. Many free blacks were employed as laborers in industry or in the busy ports along the

Atlantic coast. Others worked as domestic servants, or ran small businesses such as bakeries, tailor shops, or hairdressing salons.

Slave or free, the generations of black people did not entirely forget their African culture. Traditional legends were adapted into folktales. African music shaped the spirituals sung in black churches. A "Black English" dialect evolved, which reflected African words and ways of speech, and some words passed into standard English. (The "juke" of "jukebox" probably comes from the West African *joog*, meaning "rowdy" or "wicked"; the vegetable "okra" from *nkru-ma*; and "gumbo," a thick soup, from the Angolan *kingombo*.)

NEW FRANCE

While British colonies were spreading along the Atlantic coast, France was also competing for the wealth of the New World. French explorers sailed up the St. Lawrence River in southern Canada (their crews included a few black sailors and at least one black interpreter), and during the 1600s the colonies of New France slowly grew along the shores of the river. But although France eventually claimed an area all the way from Labrador (Newfoundland) to the Gulf of Mexico, the wealth of New France lay mainly in furs and fish, and slaves were never a major part of the economy.

But they were not unknown, either. There were black slaves in New France by 1608. The first record of a slave arriving directly from Africa dates from 1628; he was six years old, and was sold the next year for fifty half-crowns. In 1689 the French king, Louis XIV, gave the colonists permission to keep slaves (slavery was forbidden in France itself), but warned that coming from a hot climate, Africans might not survive the icy

While the residents of Upper and Lower Canada found slavery convenient and fashionable, it was not essential to the economy. As a result, slaves were rarely treated as harshly as they were in the huge work gangs of the plantations farther south.

winters. Perhaps for this reason, or perhaps just because they were considered more fashionable, the majority of slaves in New France were natives. By 1760 there were about 3,600 slaves in the colony, mostly around Montreal and mostly working as domestic help or in the dockyards. Of these, about 1,100 were black; the rest were Indian or Inuit.

THE END OF NEW FRANCE

In 1760, the British conquered New France; three years later, as part of a war settlement, France had to give up almost all its North American colonies. Now the farms and colonies that stretched along the St. Lawrence belonged to the British Empire. But part of the agreement was that the status of slaves—whether black or native—would not be changed. As British soldiers hung up their famous red coats and became settlers—as shiploads of immigrants set out to build homes and clear farms in the newly British territories of Upper and Lower Canada—one of the rights they held was to buy and sell slaves.

The Winds of Change

⊷═◉ ◉═⊷

One summer evening you pass the main house and you hear your master arguing with somebody. He sounds furious.

"Free the slaves? I never heard such a fool idea! How d'you think you'd get the crops in? How'd you get anything done? It'd be the ruination of the country."

"But how can we talk about human equality when we have slaves in our own houses?" The voice is so soft you can barely catch the words. "How can we kneel before God and pray for mercy when we ——"

"Keep up this nonsense and you'll be praying for mercy, all right. Preacher or no preacher, you'll find yourself at the wrong end of a rope!"

Even though slavery was widely accepted by white society, there had always been some whites who denounced it as inhuman and immoral, and wanted to see it abolished (ended). During the 1700s, more and more people joined the "abolitionist" cause.

Great changes were taking place in the way Europeans—and their descendants across the Atlantic—looked at the world. The old system of

(opposite) "Am I Not a Man and a Brother?" This dramatic design was used to illustrate an anti-slavery pamphlet. It was also sold as a cameo by Josiah Wedgwood, founder of Britain's famous Wedgwood pottery company.

government, feudalism, where the peasant obeyed the squire, the squire obeyed the lord, and the lord obeyed the king, was beginning to give way to a new system, democracy, in which common people take part in government by voting. The major churches, which for years had defined what was right and what was wrong, were losing worshipers to a host of small, new religions. As the spread of printing presses made books and newspapers available, many more people were learning to read and write, and exploring fresh, radical ideas. The old nobility was losing power to the rising middle classes — people like shopkeepers, craftsmen, and teachers — who were becoming more educated and prosperous. One way and another, the belief was spreading that individuals had the right to think for themselves, and to run their own lives.

THE PEOPLE TAKE CHARGE

In 1775, the thirteen British colonies from New Hampshire to Georgia rebelled against England and went to war to create an independent country, the United States of America. The new country rejected the idea of a king or queen who rules the land in favor of democracy, proclaiming in its Declaration of Independence "that all men are created equal, that they are endowed by their Creator with certain unalienable rights, that among these are Life, Liberty and the pursuit of Happiness." In 1789, the people of France overthrew their monarchy in a bloody revolution that saw the king and queen and many of their supporters beheaded on the guillotine; the slogan of the rebellion was "Liberty, Fraternity, Equality." Although a king still ruled in England, he was a "constitutional monarch" — in 1689 a bill had been passed to limit the monarch's power and make the elected

Parliament the real ruler. With all this fervor for individual rights and independence, how could anyone still defend slavery?

THE QUAKER CONNECTION

In the United States, early opposition to slavery had been voiced mainly in Pennsylvania, a colony dominated by "Quakers"—members of the Religious Society of Friends, who believed that all people were equal in the sight of God. Quakers were organized into "Meetings" instead of churches. As early as 1688, one Meeting had spoken out against slavery: "to bring men hither, and rob or sell them against their will, we will stand against." Other Meetings still condoned slavery—some argued that while slaves might be equal in the sight of God, that didn't make them equal in the sight of *man*. But many Quakers were deeply troubled by slavery, and were quietly pressing for change.

In 1738, Benjamin Lay, a passionate abolitionist, hid a container of red juice inside a hollow book that looked like a Bible, and warned the members of the influential Philadelphia Meeting that holding slaves was as wicked as "if you should thrust a sword through their hearts as I do through this book." With that, he whipped out a sword and stabbed it through the "Bible," spraying the meeting with "blood." Lay's dramatic charade succeeded only in outraging the Meeting.

By 1776, however, more persuasive abolitionists had won the day, and the Philadelphia Meeting pledged to disown any members who continued to own slaves. (The measure was to be brought in gradually, to let everyone adjust.) At last a definite stand had been taken. But while these Quakers were leaders in giving up slave-owning for themselves,

most were pacifists (people of peace) who did not believe in forcing their opinions on people outside their own religion. They would be faithful to their own consciences, but they were not yet prepared to join the battle for national abolition.

FIGHTING FOR FREEDOM

When the American colonies began fighting for independence in 1775, the British were determined to squash the rebellion—but to do so they needed as many soldiers as possible. Their solution was to promise freedom to any American slaves who ran away from rebel owners and fought on the British side. The strategy brought thousands of blacks to the British cause, and deprived the Americans of labor they desperately needed. It also made life difficult for the slave owners, who feared their slaves might take up arms against them at any moment.

Many free blacks joined the British side as well. There were blacks in the army, the navy, and the cavalry; blacks served as guides and

(opposite) A Quaker couple marry each other, rather than being married by a clergyman. Since Quakers believe that all people are equal in the sight of God, their religious services have no minister giving a sermon. Instead, people gather to worship silently, and anyone who feels inspired by God may speak. In the past Quakers defied the enormous gap between rich and poor by wearing plain clothing and refusing to doff their hats to their "superiors." They also addressed everyone as "thee," the friendly form of address in those days, when "you" was a term of respect used only to address "superior" people. These seem like small gestures today, but at the time many Quakers were persecuted for rejecting the class system, as well as for refusing to go to war.

messengers to British officers who didn't know the territory; and blacks farmed the plantations that had been taken over by British troops.

Some blacks believed so strongly in the principles of equality and independence that they supported the new American nation, even though it allowed slavery. One youth, James Forten, served in the American navy. When captured by the British and offered his freedom, he refused. He chose to be a prisoner rather than betray his country.

The British lost the war, and then their promise to free their slave soldiers was not so easily kept; the victorious Americans demanded that their slaves be returned to them. After much arguing and stalling, most runaways who had actually fought for Britain were freed, but many who had supported the British in less direct ways found themselves back in slavery. Those who were freed had to leave American soil, or risk being seized by their previous owners.

THE LOYALISTS

Although America had won its independence, some Americans were still loyal to Britain, and wanted to live on British soil. Since the British needed settlers, they promised free land and other rewards to any "Loyalists" who would move to the Maritimes (the area that now includes Nova Scotia, New Brunswick, and Prince Edward Island) or other British colonies. Of the 30,000 Loyalists who moved north to the Maritimes to claim their reward, some were wealthy landowners or military officers. Some were white farmers or tradesmen. Some were Native Americans. About 3,500 were free blacks. (There were also about 1,500 slaves belonging to the Loyalists—no one had ever offered *them* freedom.)

But when the government in the Maritimes began giving out land, the best properties were given to Loyalists who had had high military rank or large properties at home. Two-thirds of the blacks were given nothing at all, and the others got only small pieces of poor, rocky land. Although the free blacks had to pay taxes, they were not allowed to vote, and they were treated badly in many other ways.

In 1792, discouraged by their poverty and unjust treatment, and afraid that they might yet be returned to slavery, many of the black Loyalists sailed to Sierra Leone, on the west coast of Africa, in hopes of building a free black colony. Others remained in the Maritimes, however, and their presence there helped to bring about the end of slavery in the region.

Black Loyalists had also crossed into Canada around Windsor and Niagara, Ontario, and settled along the lakes and rivers. There were blacks in Butler's Rangers, a unit of commando soldiers stationed in Fort Niagara in case of American invasion, and when the unit was disbanded in 1783, many of the Rangers settled along the shore of Lake Erie. The black population was small, but across the young Canadian colonies — in villages, on farms, or working along the roads and waterways — there were free blacks building a new life and a new country.

THE TURNING OF THE TIDE

In the years after the American Revolution, the move toward abolition grew steadily stronger in the northern states. Slavery was clearly against the principles on which the new country had been built — and for most northerners, giving up slaves (if indeed they had any) was only a small inconvenience and expense. As free blacks became more conspicuous in society — building successful businesses, opening schools and churches, founding newspapers — it became harder for whites to dismiss them as "inferior." One by one, the northern states outlawed slavery in their territories. In 1807 the United States made it illegal to bring more slaves in from outside the country. But slaves could still be traded within the slave-owning states, and there was a thriving trade in smuggling them into the country illegally, as well.

In the southern states the abolitionists were less successful. While laws were passed to give slaves slightly better conditions, the South had no intention of giving up slavery. The hard fact was that the southerners' economy — in fact, their whole way of life — depended on slaves. The more the slavery system was threatened, the more passionately the pro-slavers defended the system.

The plantations' dependence on slave labor had actually increased since the 1793 invention of the cotton gin, a machine that made it easier to produce cotton. Cotton was a very popular product, and the climate in the South was ideal for growing it — but cotton crops took a lot of work, and depended on plenty of cheap labor. The more cotton the South planted, the more the South needed slavery. How would they live, the southerners argued, if they gave up their slaves? For that matter, how would their ex-slaves live? They might be free, but they would all starve together. If abolitionism was a dispute over moral philosophy in the North, in the South it was a bitter struggle for survival.

Slaves on the cotton plantations had to pick a certain weight of cotton every day, under the hot southern sun. If they failed, they were severely punished. Sometimes they fooled the overseers by slipping stones into the cotton bags, to make them heavier. One woman couldn't pick her 150-pound (about 70 kilograms) quota of cotton, and ran away into the woods instead. "I slept on logs. I had moss for a pillow. . . . I could hear bears, wild-cats, panthers, and every thing. I would come across all kinds of snakes — moccasin, blue runner, and rattlesnakes — and got used to them." She begged a little food when the overseers weren't watching, and when the nights were cold she curled up beside the chimney on a neighbor's plantation. Sometimes runaways stayed in the woods for years.

Nat Turner, a slave in the cotton fields of Virginia, had taught himself to read and write. He was deeply religious, and he had a vision telling him that God had chosen him to lead other slaves to freedom. In 1831, Turner led an uprising in which some sixty whites were killed, and he and more than seventy followers set out to capture the county seat of government. They never got there. The uprising was crushed and sixteen of his followers were executed. Turner escaped for six weeks, but was finally caught and hanged. His attempt to find freedom for his people resulted only in even stricter laws about slaves; it also put an end to the organized abolition movement in the South.

SLAVERY IN THE BRITISH EMPIRE

In Britain, as in the northern United States, slave-owning had no great economic benefits to cloud the moral issues. There, too, religion was a major
force for abolition. England's first organized anti-slavery movement had
started with a Quaker resolution in 1724. In 1772, John Wesley, founder of
the Methodist Church, cried out against "that execrable sum of all villainies
commonly called the slave trade." That year, one of Wesley's followers took
a case to court to test the laws on slavery. James Somerset, a slave from
Jamaica, had come to England with his owner and then claimed his
freedom. The case was decided by the Lord Chief Justice, who ruled that
slaves could not exist in England. "Every man who comes to England," he
declared, "is entitled to the protection of English law, whatever oppression
he may heretofore have suffered, and whatever may be the color of his
skin"—or, as a later writer put it, "The air of England is too pure to be
breathed by a slave." That legal decision gave immediate freedom to James
Somerset, and to some fourteen thousand other slaves in the country.

But although slave-*owning* had been banned in England, it was still
legal for the English to take part in the international slave trade. The abolitionists set out to change that as well, but they met heavy opposition.
The foreign slave trade employed thousands of British sailors, created a
generous market for trade goods in Africa, and supplied workers for rich
plantations in Britain's colonies. The propaganda was fierce, with pamphlets and petitions flowing in all directions. One pro-slavery writer
argued that Africans were stupid, barbaric, lazy, unmanageable, fero-
cious, inarticulate, and murderous, and that the slaves were lucky to have
been rescued from them! While abolitionists described horrific suffering

and death on appalling slave ships, traders wrote of happy, well-fed Africans singing and dancing as their cozy ships crossed the ocean.

The arguments and obstacles seemed endless, but finally, in 1807, Parliament banned all trading and shipping of African slaves. In 1833 Parliament took the next step, and passed the Abolition Act, which decreed, in no uncertain terms, that "slavery shall be and is hereby utterly and forever abolished and declared unlawful throughout the British colonies, plantations, and possessions abroad."

In Canada, the Abolition Act had little effect, as most of the slave population had already gained freedom. There had been an increase in slavery in the 1770s and 1780s, during and after the American Revolution, when the Loyalists moved in and brought their slaves. But in Canada, the mood was clearly against slavery. In 1793, the Lieutenant-Governor of Upper Canada, John Graves Simcoe—a man firmly opposed to slavery—had passed an act to gradually eliminate slave-owning: any slave who entered the territory, by choice or by force, would become free on the spot, and children born of slaves would become free when they turned twenty-five. In New Brunswick, a lawyer named Ward Chipman, one of the province's founding fathers, helped put slavery into decline with a legal argument in defense of a slave in 1800; three years later an anti-slavery decision in Lower Canada had the same effect. Even

(opposite) After 1807, if a British ship carried slaves, the ship could be confiscated and the owner fined; the same even applied to a foreign ship, if it was in British waters. But when slave ships were being pursued, sometimes the slaves would be thrown overboard to drown so that there would be no evidence of smuggling.

"THEY'RE THROWING THE POOR FELLOWS OVERBOARD."

in areas where slavery remained legal, it was unpopular, and an owner who took a slave to court usually lost the case. By the time of the Abolition Act in 1833, there were very few Canadian slaves left to free.

Ironically, the decline of slavery in Canada had its greatest effect south of the border, in the United States. The desperate question for a runaway slave had always been where to run *to*. The American Constitution of 1787 said that any slaves who escaped to a free state had to be returned to their masters. In 1793—the same year John Graves Simcoe said slaves reaching Upper Canada would become free—the U.S. Congress passed a new law, the first Fugitive Slave Act, making it a crime for anyone in the United States to help runaway slaves or prevent their arrest. American slave owners were determined to keep their "property" from slipping away to freedom.

THE WAR OF 1812

In 1812, the United States declared war on Britain and attacked Canada (which was still a British colony). The British offered land and freedom to American blacks who would fight on the English side, as they had during the American Revolution. About two thousand blacks, mostly escaped slaves, took up the offer, fearing that if England lost the war they would find themselves back in slavery. Many fighting units included blacks, and one company—"Captain Runchey's Company of Coloured Men"—was entirely black except for its commander. This time England won the war, and the blacks kept their freedom. But when they claimed the land they had been promised, they found—once again—that it was too poor to afford them a decent living.

In 1819, the American government requested Canadian cooperation in returning any slaves who escaped to Canada, and asked if Americans could pursue escaped slaves into Canadian territory to recover them. Although the diplomatic situation was an awkward one, the Canadians refused; any slave who managed to reach Canada, they insisted, would be free.

To the runaway's question "Where can I be safe?" there was at last an answer. Just as James Somerset had won his freedom by setting foot on English soil, so American slaves could now do the same by making their way across the Canadian border.

All they had to do was get there.

Runaway!

⊷⇒ ⇐⊶

You did it! You slipped away from the plantation and walked all night, following the North Star. Three times you hid in the bushes, your heart pounding, as people went by. And you swam the river, though the current almost carried you away.

But now the sun is coming up; you don't dare stay near the road. Your clothes are wet, and you ate your last bit of bread before you swam the river. You feel so cold and empty—and so alone! If only you could go to that farmhouse over there. . . . No, it's too dangerous. Better just hide in the woods and try to get some sleep, and wait for the safety of the darkness.

Wait! What was that? It sounded like . . . dogs!

Francis Henderson labored on a northern plantation from the time he was ten years old, living with his aunt in an open hut that let in the rain, and sleeping on a board propped up on a stool, with no blankets and only his jacket as a pillow. He knew that fellow slaves sometimes escaped, but he

(opposite) In North America, the North Star (also called the Pole Star, or Polaris) appears to hang almost directly over the North Pole, so if you follow it, you will be going almost straight north. To find it, follow the line from the two stars at the pouring end of the Big Dipper (right); the North Star is at the upper left.

couldn't figure out how they did it. "Men would disappear all at once: a man who was working by me yesterday would be gone today—how, I knew not. I really believed that they had some great flying machine to take them through the air." How did runaways know where to go? How could they ever find their way to Canada? They weren't allowed to meet freely with other slaves, to hear about escape routes. Most of them couldn't read, so they couldn't pass written messages or maps. Their owners were careful not to let them hear any talk that would help them get to freedom; indeed, many owners tried to frighten their slaves with tall tales, saying that Canada was a barren land where nothing except rice would grow, that it was full of wild geese who could scratch your eyes out, and that abolitionists were really cannibals who ate anyone who turned to them for help!

But the lure of freedom was powerful, and slowly—in whispers, from mouth to mouth—word got around that escape *was* possible. A slave who reached the free states in the North could hide among free blacks, and could with luck avoid recapture. A slave who reached the distant and mysterious land of Canada could be free—truly and legally free. The trip would be difficult and dangerous, but the reward was overwhelming. Many slaves made up their minds to run away.

But it wasn't easy to escape. Slaves were valuable property, and they were watched closely. Many couldn't leave their homes without written permission. Once they were on the road, they were suspected by anyone who saw them. In some places they weren't allowed to ride trains or even cross bridges without a written pass. A slave riding a horse on the open road was assumed to have stolen it. Even carrying food or clothing was dangerous, as it suggested that you weren't on your way

This American painting by Eastman Johnson, called A Ride for Liberty — The
Fugitive Slaves, *shows a couple escaping with a small child. In fact, many runaways
had to leave their families behind, and hope to be reunited with them later. It was just
too difficult and dangerous to arrange a family escape.*

home. So most fugitives had to travel by night, on foot, with nothing to
eat but the scraps they could find or steal as they went. And all the way,
they knew they might be stopped, searched, questioned, and even
seized, at any moment.

Escaping slaves were chased by professional slave hunters, who pursued them with tracking dogs. The hunters tried to shoot the runaways with birdshot (small bullets), to catch them without doing too much damage to this "valuable property." Indeed, one slave was caught wearing a homemade "bulletproof vest" stuffed with turkey feathers. But if the dogs sometimes caught up with the runaways first, and tore them apart, that was fine with the owners — it would give the rest of the slaves something to think about.

THE WATCHERS AND THE HUNTERS

There were many eyes watching out for runaways. Of course, any good citizen was expected to report them and have them arrested. But there were also "patrols," gangs of poor whites who made their living by riding the roads and chasing down fugitives, to collect the rewards for them. These predatory bands were famous for their cruelty. Philip Younger, a slave from Alabama, described them:

> the patrols go out in companies at about dark, and ride nearly all night. If they meet a colored man without a pass, it is [by law] thirty-nine lashes; but they don't stop for the law, and if they tie a man up, he is very well off if he gets only two hundred.

Runaways might be locked up in a place called "the cage"—one black described it as a "hog-hole"—until their angry owners paid a fine and took them home for more punishment.

Francis Henderson said that in the North, the patrols would hang around the homes of free blacks, hoping to catch them helping a runaway—and described how the tables were sometimes turned:

> I have known the slaves to stretch clothes lines across the street, high enough to let the horse pass but not the rider; then the boys would run, and the patrols in full chase would be thrown off by running against the lines.

Not all the hunters were human. As soon as slaves disappeared, dogs would be sent out after them. If the owners didn't have dogs of their own, they could call in slave catchers who made their living by using bloodhounds and other hunting dogs to track down fugitives. The dogs would follow for days, sniffing their way along the track and baying with excitement as they got closer and closer.

LIVING IN THE SHADOWS

Some slaves—especially women—ran off and hid, but couldn't bear to go far away and leave their families behind. One young woman had been promised a terrible beating for daring to strike back when her mistress hit her. She escaped into the woods, where her husband fixed up a cave for her. He lined the floor with pine needles, made furniture out of pine logs, and even put in a stove, with a stovepipe running into the swamp, though they could use it only at night for fear somebody might see the smoke. There she stayed, with her husband joining her as often as he dared. She bore three children in the cave, with only her husband to help her, and she didn't leave until they were all freed seven years later.

FOLLOWING THE STAR

But most slaves kept heading north, following the North Star and whatever scraps of directions they had heard. One of them, a woman from Mississippi (we don't know her name), was determined to make the long trip to Canada—a distance of about 900 miles (1,400 kilometers). She had no map and no clear directions. All she knew was that she had to go along the Mississippi River for a long way, and then cross it and follow the North Star. But she was deeply religious, and she trusted God to help her find her way. She bundled up a little food and clothing and set off late at night, heading into the swamps and forests. For days she traveled, hearing the dogs baying on her track, and crossing streams wherever she could to throw them off the scent. But then she heard the hounds catching up with her, and there was nowhere to hide, and no river to cross. As the snarling pack closed in on her, she fell to her knees and begged God to save her. Then she stood and faced the dogs and, on a sudden inspiration, took the last crumbs of food from her pocket and held them out. Instead of attacking her, the dogs licked the crumbs from her hands, and bounded away.

The woman dropped to her knees again and promised God that if she got to Canada alive, she would spend the rest of her days doing his good works. She traveled for months, hiding by day, living on scraps of fruits and vegetables, wading through shallow rivers and building rafts to paddle across deep ones. When she reached the free state of Illinois, some kind people helped her get to Detroit, where someone else ferried her across the river into Canada and freedom. All we know of her after that is that she spent the rest of her life doing good deeds, keeping her promise to God.

Two slaves from Virginia, John Taylor and Monroe Evans, were so brutally treated that they ran away. But the dogs soon caught up with them, and they were taken back and savagely whipped. A few months later they ran away again, and got as far as Tennessee—but again they were taken back and punished. This time, though, the overseer was determined to put an end to their escapes. He fitted both men with iron collars that held three bells high over their heads. They were watched

closely all day, and at night they were handcuffed and locked in a special pen. There seemed to be no way out.

Then one day one of the men managed to sneak a file out of a tool chest and into his pocket, and that night they set out to free themselves. Because every movement set the bells ringing, they had to begin by muffling the sound. They did this by tearing up a blanket with their teeth, and stuffing the scraps into the bells—a slow and awkward process in handcuffs. Then, since the man with the file in his pocket couldn't reach it because of the handcuffs, the other man had to wriggle around and work the file out. At last they were able to begin the slow work of filing through the handcuffs and the collars, and before morning they were over the walls and away.

After walking for several weeks, they were almost ambushed by a patrol at a covered bridge. But they spotted it in time, and Taylor managed to creep so close to the slave hunters that he could overhear their plans. After avoiding the patrol, they were lucky enough to find a steamer sailing to Cincinnati, and slept among the cotton bales as it

---

(opposite) Some runaways rubbed their feet with onions or spruce gum to try to confuse the dogs. But the best way to make them lose the scent was by traveling through water. If there were no rivers or streams handy, many slaves headed for swamps, risking alligators and deadly snakes, and putting up with all kinds of biting insects. Sometimes, when escape seemed too dangerous, the runaways stayed in the swamp for years. In Dismal Swamp, on the border between Virginia and North Carolina, almost two thousand escaped slaves kept themselves alive by hunting, fishing, and stealing. It was a miserable life, but it was better than what they had left behind.

---

carried them north. In Cincinnati they tried to buy a pair of shoes, and were alarmed when the shopkeeper guessed that they were runaways. But this was the North, where slaves had many sympathizers; the shopkeeper gave them the shoes as a gift, and directed them to a free black who would help them. John Taylor and Monroe Evans reached Canada and freedom, but they bore the marks of the whip and the handcuffs for the rest of their lives.

Many fugitives managed to cover part of their long voyage by boat. When John Jackson was a young man in South Carolina, he had a new wife and baby son whom he adored. His mean overseer was so jealous of his happiness that he told John he was going to marry off John's wife to another slave. (Most slave marriages were personal arrangements, with no legal protection.) John Jackson resolved to escape and then come back and spirit his family away. He made his way to Charleston, about 100 miles (160 kilometers) away, and hid in the hold of a sailing ship. After a week he was so hungry and thirsty that he had to come out, but fortunately the ship's captain was a good man, and took him to Boston. Jackson reached Canada, and eventually moved to England, but he never saw his family again. When he got someone to write home for him, he discovered that his wife had indeed been married to the other slave. She had died shortly after, and the baby too.

Francis Henderson — the slave who imagined "flying machines" when he was a boy — escaped to freedom as well. When he was nineteen he began asking around for information on how to get away, and luckily "happened to ask in the right quarter." Soon he joined fifteen others on the road to safety.

As for Philip Younger, he spent most of his life in slavery — in the deep south of Alabama, where he lived, escape was almost impossible. But by the time he was fifty-five he had saved enough money to buy freedom for himself and his wife. "Old as I am," he said when he was seventy-two, "I would rather face the Russian fire, or die at the point of the sword, than go into slavery."

CROSSING TO THE PROMISED LAND

Ever since 1793, when the government of Upper Canada decreed that any slave entering the territory automatically became free, fugitive slaves had been making their way across the border. But it wasn't easy; while there were many shaded and twisting paths through the farms and forests of the northern states, there were only a few places to get around the oceanlike expanses of the Great Lakes. Slave hunters knew that, and kept a sharp eye on the towns around Niagara Falls, New York, and Detroit, Michigan, as well as the ships that sailed from there.

There were a few places where it was possible to swim across, and in winter it was sometimes even possible to walk across the ice. But most runaways made the crossing on a vessel of some kind, whether it was a rough and tippy homemade raft or a commercial steamship.

FRIENDS IN NEED

Probably every slave who ever escaped had help from somebody. Sometimes the help was very slight: someone at home might notice the preparations for escape but say nothing; someone along the road might offer a bit of food, or give directions; a town dweller might warn the runaway that *this* road was safer from patrols than *that* one. Other times the help was more substantial: someone would offer a hiding place for a few days, or a rowboat ride across a river, although anyone caught helping a slave escape could be punished.

DIGBY, 21ſt JUNE 1792.

RUN AWAY, Joſeph Odel and Peter Lawrence (Negroes) from their Maſters, and left Digby laſt evening, the firſt mentioned is about Twenty four years of Age, five Feet ſix Inches high, had on a light brown Coat, red Waiſtcoat and thickſet Breeches, but took other Cloaths with him, he is a likely young Fellow with remarkable white Teeth.— The other is about five Feet eight Inches high, very Black had on lighteſh coloured Clothes.—Whoever will ſecure ſaid Negroes ſo that their Maſters may have them again, ſhall receive TEN DOLLARS Reward, and all reaſonable Charges paid.

DANIEL ODEL,
PHILLIP EARL.

Slaves who escaped their immediate pursuers were still not safe. Newspaper advertisements like this one — from Nova Scotia's Royal Gazette in 1792 — offered rewards to anyone who happened to spot them — and two hundred years ago, ten dollars was a lot of money.

One ex-slave who escaped to Canada, John Warren, noted wryly that "the white folks down south don't seem to sleep much, nights. They are watching for runaways, and to see if any other slave comes among theirs, or theirs go off among others. They listen and peep to see if anything has been stolen, and to find if anything is going on. 'What is there in this barrel? Too many d****d barrels in here, — I'll have'm put out!'"

The people who helped the runaways were of all races and religions. There were slaves among them, and free blacks, and whites, and Native Americans; there were Catholics, Protestants, Jews, and many others. Some were fierce abolitionists who detested slavery and would face any danger if it meant helping a slave toward freedom. Others weren't sure whether slavery was right or wrong, but found themselves involved by accident, and helped the slaves on an impulse of kindness or pity.

But as word spread among the slaves that escape was possible, that there was freedom to be found in the North, the people helping runaways began to be more organized. If one farm family along the way let slaves sleep in their barn, they would know where the fugitives could find shelter farther down the road. If kindly people living near a river noticed that runaways were always caught around a certain bridge, they would have someone watch out for them, and warn them, and show them a safer way to cross. Giving help was dangerous; not only was it against the law, but it also drew the fury of slave owners, who saw as traitors those who sympathized with slaves, and sometimes took violent revenge.

All the same, as the people helping the runaways got to know who was sympathetic and who wasn't, who could be trusted and who couldn't, they became more confident. They started planning ahead, planning together, looking for safer ways to guide more runaways northward. Slowly a network of rescue was growing—a secret network of people who dared to put themselves at risk for what they knew was right. It had no one leader, no official existence, no formal organization. But it would become a legend. And—strangely enough—it would be known as the Underground Railroad.

The Railroad That Wasn't

⟵⟶

You're weak from hunger, and feeling sick; you can't go much farther. You have to ask for help, despite the risk of being caught. You hide near a field and wait till the overseer rides off, and then call quietly to the nearest slave.

"Get away, quick!" she whispers. "It's too dangerous here."

"Please, I just need a scrap of food," you beg.

"Not here! Try the house with the green roof. But wait till dark!"

You slip away, wondering who lives in the house with the green roof, and whether they'll help you. For now, all you can do is hide, and wait . . . and pray.

It was called the Underground Railroad, but it had no engines and no trains. It had stations but no tracks. Its passengers traveled without tickets, and its conductors blew no whistles. So why was it called a railroad?

(opposite) Slaves at home on a southern plantation. In some places slaves couldn't even be given their freedom. As early as 1663, Maryland declared that anyone who was a slave there was a slave for life. In 1818, Georgia set a fine of $1,000 — an immense amount of money at that time — for anyone who freed a slave. The state of Virginia simply decreed that any freed black who remained in the state for a month was automatically a slave again. In short, the feeling was that slaves were meant to be slaves, and anything that freed them was wrong.

As the routes of the Underground Railroad converged in the north, there could be large parties of refugees arriving together, under cover of darkness. They all had to be fed and provided with safe places to rest and hide. Large groups like this one would be split up and lodged with various abolitionist families nearby, until they could safely move on. Just coordinating these groups could be a complex and worrisome task.

It's hard for us to imagine today how slowly people used to travel. Throughout most of history, trips were by foot, by boat, or by animal— whether it was a camel ambling over an Arabian desert, or a horse-drawn covered wagon lurching across the prairies. Even by stagecoach, a trip of sixty miles (about 100 kilometers) took several days each way. Today we can drive that far and back and be home in time for lunch.

In the 1830s, steam-powered trains first appeared in North America—trains that could travel farther in an hour than a horse could go in a day. The surest, fastest, easiest way to make a long trip was by train. So when people wanted to describe a network that seemed to pick runaways up and whisk them off to freedom, they naturally compared it to a train—a mysterious secret railroad. Since "underground" means hidden and out of sight, they called it the Underground Railroad.

WHAT WAS THE RAILROAD MADE UP OF?

There were no metal tracks in the Underground Railroad; it moved along pathways, river crossings, and a fellowship of goodwill and sympathy. The *conductors* were people who met fugitive slaves—*passengers*—and guided them along their way, giving them directions, leading them on foot or by horse, or smuggling them in carts and carriages. The *stations* were places where runaways could stop and rest, getting a meal and a night's sleep, and perhaps fresh clothing or other help. A station might be a barn or a church, a lonely farmhouse or a secret room in a fashionable town home. Stations were run by *stationmasters*. Conductors and station-masters were often free blacks or poor farmers, but they could also be wealthy, well-known citizens.

Although there were individuals helping fugitive blacks from the beginning, the Underground Railroad first became organized in the early 1800s. It never really functioned in the Deep South—there just weren't enough sympathizers there, and anyone caught helping runaways was likely to be savagely punished. But if slaves could make their own way to the northern slave states, like Missouri, Kentucky, and Virginia, they had a good chance of finding help for the trip across the Mason-Dixon line (the boundary between north and south), through the free states, and into Canada—if they decided to go that far. After 1826, when Canada formally refused to return runaways to the United States, much of the Underground Railroad led toward Windsor and Niagara Falls, Ontario, where crossing into Canada was easiest. There were many *terminals*, where refugees were welcomed and fed and given temporary accommodation, along the Canadian shore of Lake Erie and around Niagara and Windsor.

HOW DID THE UNDERGROUND RAILROAD STAY HIDDEN?

Everything was done as secretly and confusingly as possible. Pathways might zigzag and cut through streams, and even double back on themselves. Routes were often changed at the last moment, in case word had got out. And there were "wild-goose chase" routes as well: when a slave hunter came looking for his prey, he would be assured that *that very slave* had *just* gone *this* way, when the runaway had gone the opposite way days earlier!

The escaping slaves might be dressed in disguises, or given farm tools to carry. They might be hidden in wagonloads of goods, or even inside secret compartments built into carriages or wagons. Because people were sometimes caught and searched, messages were often passed in code. Runaways were referred to as packages or merchandise; a conductor or stationmaster who had a message that "by Tuesday you should receive a shipment of four large kegs of dark ale and one small one" would prepare for the arrival of four adults and a child.

*If the slave hunters couldn't find runaways, they would seize free blacks instead —
often children — and falsely accuse them of having escaped. Then they would take
them south and sell them for whatever they could get. No black could ever feel entirely
safe from these ruthless kidnappers.*

Some of the most common messages were passwords—secret words that let runaways and conductors recognize each other when they had never met before. There were code names for towns and people. And there were also discreet signals: a light in a specific window of a station, or a cloth or flag hanging in a certain place, would reassure a fugitive that it was safe to come to the door. Or runaways might be told to announce their presence with a special knock or birdcall.

Some stations had secret rooms where fugitives could hide from their pursuers. Others had concealed doors, or even tunnels, so that they could enter or escape unseen. The Episcopal Parish House in Maine provided respectable religious camouflage for a station, as did the Touro Synagogue in Rhode Island, the country's oldest Jewish house of worship.

In an era when women were often considered weak and timid, many slave-hunting men couldn't believe that a "mere woman" could outdo them. The women made the most of that mistake. A woman in Ohio was carrying fugitives in her cart, hidden under a quilt, when the cart became stuck in deep mud. She calmly asked for help from some passing men—all firm pro-slavers—and stood "helplessly" by while they rocked and shoved and grunted till the cart was free. Another woman used to send runaways through a trapdoor in the floor that led to a hiding place, then she would pull a rug and rocking chair over the trapdoor, and sit placidly rocking while the slave hunters searched around her.

Yet another woman saved Charley, a slave from Virginia, when his owner was hot on his footsteps. Charley had been told to hide in the back of a house, but when he got there he found a sick woman lying helplessly in bed with a small baby:

I heard horses running up the road, and looking out, saw my master and another man coming. I began to cry, but she told me to get under the bed and lie still, and when I had done so she took up her baby, and got it to screaming with all its might. Soon master opened the door and looked in, and asked if a negro boy had come in there. The baby cried and she pretended to try to stop it, and asked him what he wanted. He repeated the question. She tried to hush the baby, and finally said, "Husband is at the barn; he can tell you if he has been here."

The minute Charley's owner headed for the barn, the woman sent Charley up a ladder to the loft, where he hid until his owner gave up and rode away.

There were also women who took a more hands-on approach to slave catchers — like the tavern-keeper's daughter who fought one off with a broom, the elegant lady who clipped one in the head with a well-aimed stone (apparently she found him ill-bred), and the farm wife who drove them away with boiling water and a pitchfork.

All these tricks and secrets and adventures may make the Underground Railroad sound like a game. But in fact it was a dangerous business, not only for the escaping slaves but for those who helped them, too.

COMPROMISE AND CONFLICT

Ever since the original Thirteen Colonies had broken away from Britain in the 1770s, the United States had been expanding. As settlers kept

Supporters of slavery were infuriated by the anti-slavery movement. In 1835, an angry mob broke into a post office in South Carolina, ransacked the mail, and burned all the abolitionist newspapers they could find. Many southern postmasters used this as an excuse to ban the mailing of anti-slavery papers.

spreading west and south, farming new territories and founding new towns, one by one the territories applied to become states. The abolitionists (who were mainly in the North) would have liked all the new states to be free of the terrible blight of slavery. But the southern, slaveholding states were afraid of being outnumbered by free states; they feared that sooner or later they would be forced to give up their slaves, and the rich plantations that depended on them.

So every time a new state joined the union, there was a political battle over whether the state would be free or slaveholding. In 1820, when there were as many slave states as free states, there was a bitter fight over whether Missouri could be a slaveholding state. Finally, in a decision called the Missouri Compromise, Missouri was made slaveholding but Maine was admitted as a free state at the same time, to keep the numbers even. In 1850, there was such a furious debate over whether slavery would be allowed in Texas, California, Utah, and New Mexico that the southern states threatened to break away and form their own country. That argument was finally resolved by a complicated settlement called the Compromise of 1850, which really didn't satisfy anyone. Just four years later there was another desperate struggle, this time over the great area that is now Kansas and Nebraska. With each confrontation, tempers grew hotter on both sides.

There was a second reason why the southerners were worried about being surrounded by free states. Not only would it put more pressure on them to eventually give up their slaves, but it would also give their escaped slaves more places to hide. And the fact that white Americans actually *helped* the slaves escape was an outrage many southerners could hardly bear. Hiding a slave, many felt, was the same as stealing one; and if horse thieves were hanged, shouldn't slave stealers meet the same end? Virginia and North Carolina thought so — they had the death penalty for both offenses.

PUNISHING THE RESCUERS

Helping runaways was illegal even in the free states. The American Constitution had declared in 1787 that any slave who escaped to a free state had to be returned to the owner. In 1793 the first Fugitive Slave Act made it a crime to help a runaway or prevent a runaway's arrest. Part of the 1850 Compromise—the attempt to keep the South from breaking away and forming a new country—was the second Fugitive Slave Act, which ordered all "good citizens" of the United States to cooperate in catching runaways, and set heavy fines and even jail sentences for those who helped them escape.

In the southern states, the penalties had to be taken very seriously. Those who helped slaves escape were generally despised, and often the slaveholders took matters into their own hands. Once they decided someone was guilty, they didn't always worry about what the law said. In 1850 a white couple in Maryland were charged with helping runaway slaves. The court found them not guilty, but enraged slaveholders dragged them out of their home and "tarred and feathered" them— coated their bodies with hot tar, covered the tar with chicken feathers, and drove them out of town.

In the North, though, the anti-slavery feeling was strong enough that many people continued to defy the law. John Fairfield, a white southerner whose family were slave owners, made many trips as a conductor; his southern accent helped him fool suspicious slave owners. One time he slipped twenty-eight black fugitives through the streets of Cincinnati in broad daylight. How did he do it? He simply put them in the closed coaches of a phony funeral procession, and watched unsuspecting slave hunters doff their hats in respect as the runaways rolled toward freedom. Henrietta Bowers Duterte, Philadelphia's first black woman undertaker, also hid fugitives in funeral processions—sometimes inside the coffin!

After the second *Fugitive Slave Act* was passed in 1850, it became common for slave hunters to snatch blacks who had escaped to the northern states and drag them back to slavery south of the Mason-Dixon line. Abolitionists tried to protect the runaways, but if they were caught they faced severe punishment.

Laws or no laws, a black who managed to make contact with the Underground Railroad would be passed from hand to hand, with kindness, and caution, and considerable ingenuity.

CHARLEY'S STORY

Charley—the slave who was hidden by the sick woman with the baby—had stumbled onto the Underground Railroad. After his owner left, he was given food and a place to sleep till dark; then, after another meal, he was sent off through the night with two white men. Charley knew that his owner had posted a $500 reward for his capture, and assumed that the men were going to turn him in. Instead they led him to the Ohio River (the Ohio border), ferried him across in a small boat, and gave him two loaves of bread, saying, "This is a free state, and there is the North Star—God bless you."

Charley walked on, but by daylight he had lost his way and didn't know whether he was going north or south. Before long, though, he met a man who took him to a safe hiding place and brought him food. A few weeks later, when the hunt for Charley had died down, he was on his way to Buffalo, New York, and freedom.

DANIEL FISHER'S STORY

Daniel Fisher was a slave in South Carolina, where the Underground Railroad barely existed. Fisher made his escape with a friend, and the two headed north. They walked many miles, traveling by night with no food but the scraps they got from slaves along the road. Sometimes, when clouds covered the North Star, they lost their way and walked in circles.

At one river they couldn't cross without a pass, and had to wait until they could use a fisherman's boat.

When the pair reached Virginia, they were advised to stow away on a boat for the trip north. For three months they lived in the woods, in earthen dens they had dug, waiting for a chance to get on a boat. At last they managed to stow away, and after a four-day journey without food they reached Washington, D.C. There the captain of the boat fed them and gave them some loaves of bread, and pointed them in the right direction.

Their perils were not over yet. First they met a man who suspected them, and was going to turn them in, until they made up a story that fooled him. But they decided that their bread had made him suspicious, and threw the loaves away. After several days without food they came to a river, and had to walk 5 miles (8 kilometers) to find a bridge:

> We finally came to one, but on attempting to cross were stopped, as we had no passes. It was a toll bridge, and there was a woman in charge of it, who upon our payment of a penny for each and the promise to come back immediately, allowed us to go by. . . . At the other end of the bridge we were stopped again, as the gates were opened only for [slave-labor] teams. However . . . we finally managed to slip by in the shadow of a team, and—glorious thought—we were at last on the free soil of Pennsylvania!

Fisher and his friend had more close calls, but managed to get to Philadelphia, where friends took them in. They were still in danger of being captured and returned to slavery, but now they were in the heart of Underground Railroad country. The pair separated, to have less chance of being recognized, and Fisher joined a group of blacks traveling to New York. There he was put onto a steamboat going to New Haven, where a black man led him to a hotel and he was given a meal and a suit of clothes. He was given directions to a town and told what name to ask for, and after another long and weary trek he arrived at his destination. There he found friends and work and a new home. But he always disguised himself with a wig after that, and never used his real name, and he lived with the fear that someday, somehow, he might be captured and enslaved once again.

Arnold Gragston's story

Arnold Gragston was a slave in Kentucky who was asked to row a runaway across the river. At first he refused, for fear of being caught. "But then I saw the girl, and she was such a pretty little thing . . . and looking as scared as I was feeling. . . ." Finally he agreed to take the chance.

> I don't know how I ever rowed the boat across the river. The current was strong, and I was trembling. . . . We didn't dare to whisper, so I couldn't tell her how sure I was that Mr. Tabb or some of the others' owners would tear me up when they found out what I had done. I just knew they would find out. I was worried, too, about where to put her out of the boat. I couldn't ride her across the river all night, and I didn't know a thing about the other side. . . . I just knew that if I pulled the boat up and went to asking people where to take her I would get a beating or get killed.

Arnold got his passenger safely to shore, and in the next few years he crossed the river many times, ferrying several hundred people to freedom. Then he was almost caught, and he and his wife had to flee to the North.

Arnold never took payment from his passengers, and after that first night he didn't even see them, for they always traveled on moonless nights; he only knew them by a secret password. As an old man he liked to tell his thirty-one grandchildren "how their grandpa brought emancipation to loads of slaves he could touch and feel, but never could see."

"Liberty or Death"

⊷═◠ ◠═⊷

Hot soup with soda biscuits, and ham and grits, and peach cobbler — three servings! — you know it's rude to gobble up so much, but you can't stop yourself. It feels so good to eat again, and to be warm, and just to be with people. When you turn down a fourth plate of cobbler, the stationmistress shows you to a tiny basement room with four narrow beds.

"You get some sleep now. And when you wake up, just stay down here quietly; you never know who's around. We'll come and get you when it's time to leave."

"But where do I go from here?" you ask.

"Oh, you're in luck. There's a certain somebody coming through here who's very brave and clever, and knows the way well. I don't like to use names — but believe me, you'll be in the best of hands."

(opposite) Laura Haviland's outfit is a good example of the modest Quaker costume. Haviland served the Underground Railroad as both a stationmaster and a conductor, and also started a school that taught blacks and whites, boys and girls, together — a revolutionary idea at the time. Here she holds iron shackles and a "knee-stiffener," used to keep slaves from running away; beneath her foot is an iron slave-collar. Later she moved to Windsor, Ontario, where she taught school and organized a "Union Church" to serve ex-slaves of all denominations.

While some runaways spent the rest of their lives in cautious secrecy, others were openly celebrated for their daring and ingenious escapes. They gave speeches at public meetings, helping to raise support and money for the abolitionist cause. They were interviewed by abolitionist newspapers, and described in books. Their

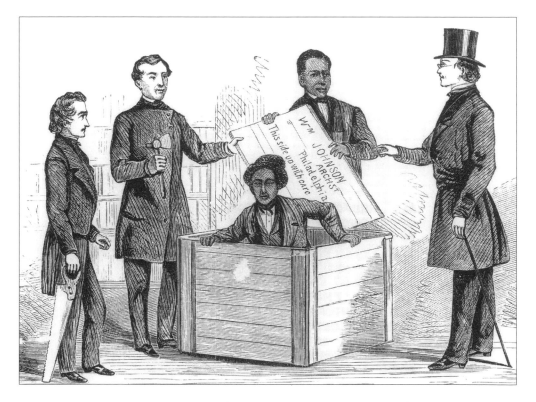

Henry "Box" Brown emerges triumphantly to greet members of the Philadelphia Anti-Slavery Society. One of the black members present was William Still, a conductor who took the time to write down the stories of these daring escapes. In 1872, after slavery had been abolished, Still published a book called Underground Railroad Records. *Without him, many of these adventures would have been lost.*

stories were carried back to the slave states and passed from plantation to plantation, encouraging other slaves to make the dangerous trip north.

HENRY "BOX" BROWN

Henry Brown, a slave in Virginia, decided that the perils of patrols and bloodhounds were not for him; since he was treated like a white man's property, he would *travel* like a white man's property. He had a carpenter build him a fabric-lined box just big enough to sit in — it wasn't large enough to allow him to lie down. Then he climbed in, with a few biscuits, a small supply of water, and a tool he could bore a hole with to get fresh air. The box was nailed up tight and shipped to Philadelphia.

The trip took twenty-six long and uncomfortable hours. Although the box was clearly marked This Side Up with Care, shipping workers ignored the sign, and Henry Brown traveled many miles upside down! But the "shipment" reached Philadelphia safely, and was delivered to the Anti-Slavery Society. The people there knew that a runaway was supposed to be in the box, and they half expected him to be dead from his ordeal. Nervously they pried the lid off the box. The bruised and weary occupant rose to his feet, said, "How do you do, gentlemen?," and sang a hymn—"I Waited Patiently for the Lord, and He Heard My Prayer"—to celebrate his safe arrival into freedom.

Henry was known as "Box" Brown from then on. He worked for the Underground Railroad, was a popular speaker at antislavery meetings, and even had a song written about his bold escape.

Ellen Craft in her disguise as a white southern gentleman, but with the bandages removed from her face. A fellow passenger who questioned her "slave" — really her husband, William — was told that the "young master" suffered from rheumatism and toothache, and was on his way to consult a famous doctor.

WILLIAM AND ELLEN CRAFT

The Crafts were a young married couple who were owned by different masters. Since they lived in Georgia, too far south for the Underground Railroad, they had to arrange their own escape. The plan they came up with was breathtakingly daring: they would travel together, in broad daylight, by steamboat and by train. But while William would go as a black slave, Ellen would disguise herself as a rich young *white man*.

Luckily, Ellen's skin was light enough to fool people. In a good black suit and boots with tall heels, she could carry herself like a young man. Her hair would have to be cut, and green-tinted glasses would help conceal her eyes. But how could they hide her soft, beardless face? The "gentleman" would have to have a toothache, and muffle his face in a large bandage. If he limped and carried a cane, that would cover up any oddness in his walk. He had better be hard of hearing, since Ellen couldn't risk a conversation. And since she didn't know how to read or write — to register at hotels and sign papers — the gentleman would have to have a sore arm, and wear a sling. All in all, this young gentleman was so pathetically infirm that it was no wonder his faithful slave had to stay by his side all the way to Philadelphia!

The Crafts had a nerve-racking trip with many close calls along the way. One evening on the steamboat, Ellen found herself sitting right next to the captain at dinner, and he warned her to keep a sharp eye on her slave in case he tried to run away! Finally they reached freedom, and their thrilling story made them heroes to the anti-slavery movement.

"Moses"

Harriet Tubman was a slave in Maryland who had been worked cruelly since she was six years old. When she was about twenty-eight, she learned that she was going to be sold, and might never see her family again. She was determined not to let this happen, no matter what risks she had to take. That very night, she packed a scrap of bread and salt herring into a kerchief and slipped off the plantation.

Harriet hardly knew which way to turn, but she decided to take a chance, and go to a white woman on a nearby farm who had often spoken to her kindly. Would the woman help her? The answer was yes — the woman gave her directions to another house, a station on the Underground

Railroad. It took Harriet all night to walk to this second house, but when she got there she was given a meal, and the next night she was hidden in a wagonload of produce and driven to the river. She was to follow the river, she was told; she was to hide by day, and stay off the roads even at night, because the patrols were looking for her.

In the course of her escape, Harriet passed from one hiding place to another: the attic of a Quaker farm, the haystack of a German family, and even the earthen potato cellar in the cabin of a free black family. But at last she reached Philadelphia, got a job as a hotel cook, and met other fugitives who told her of their escapes, and the families they had had to leave behind.

A couple of years later, Harriet got word that her sister Mary and her two children were going to be sold off the plantation. Although Mary was married to a free black, he could not legally save his wife and family from being sent away; all he could do was ask the Underground Railroad to help them. A plan had been set up, but one more conductor was still needed, to lead the family from Baltimore to Philadelphia. Harriet volunteered. Her friends tried to change her mind, arguing that the mission was too dangerous, but Harriet insisted: she would travel back into the slave states to bring her loved ones out. She succeeded, and after that she went back again and again, bringing out other relatives—including her elderly parents—and strangers too.

"I think slavery is the next thing to hell," said Harriet Tubman. "If a person would send another into bondage, he would, it appears to me, be bad enough to send him into hell, if he could." She led so many people out of that hell and into the "Promised Land" of freedom that she was nicknamed "Moses," after the prophet in the Bible who led the Jews out of slavery to the Promised Land of Canaan.

When the second Fugitive Slave Act was passed in 1850, giving slave hunters the right to snatch back runaways even in the North, Harriet was no longer safe in Philadelphia. She moved to Canada and made her home in St. Catharines, Ontario, near the American border. But she remained dedicated to her mission, making a rescue trip

Harriet Tubman, called "Moses" because she led so many slaves to freedom. Her cool courage was legendary. Once she had to pass through the village where her previous owner lived. She bought some live chickens and hobbled through town as though she were very old. When she spotted her previous owner, she "dropped" the chickens, and put on a great show of trying to catch them. All the bystanders, including the owner, laughed so hard at the "clumsy old woman" that they never even recognized her.

every spring and every fall, and working in hotels between her trips, to raise money for them. She knew how dangerous it was—there was a huge reward of $12,000 for her capture—and she always carried a gun. She was famous for her strength and endurance, and her unwavering faith in God. As she herself said, talking about her original escape,

> I had reasoned this out in my mind; there was one of two things I had a *right* to, liberty or death; if I could not have one, I would have the other; for no man should take me alive. . . .

She never was captured, and she never lost a passenger. Harriet Tubman continued her personal campaign, by working as a conductor and by making public speeches, until slavery was abolished throughout the United States.

Songs of freedom

Many slave owners liked to hear their slaves singing religious songs, because they figured that a slave who found comfort in God and the promise of heaven was less likely to be a "troublemaker" here on earth. The slaves took advantage of this, and many spiritual songs had double meanings. "Canaan" could sound a lot like "Canada," and someone who sang about "crossing over" to the "Promised Land" might be thinking of the Ohio River rather than the hereafter. A slave idly humming "Go Down Moses" might be passing a message that Harriet Tubman was in the neighborhood.

One famous song advised listeners to "follow the drinking gourd" to where an old man was waiting—"left foot, peg leg." It promised that the riverbank was a good road and the dead trees would point the way, and warned that beyond the first river lay a second one. The "drinking gourd" was a code name for the Big Dipper, which pointed to the North Star. The "old man" was a conductor with a wooden "peg leg." The first river was the Little Tombigbee, and the second was the Ohio — the border of the free states.

Alexander Ross was a doctor from Belleville, Ontario, who made regular trips to the southern states for "bird-watching." He was welcomed by plantation owners, but at night he would slip out and give their slaves directions to Canada, passing out knives, compasses, and a little money to those who planned to escape. Once, after Ross helped a slave named Joe escape, he was seized and arrested for the crime. He was about to be convicted — and severely punished — when Joe walked into the courtroom and explained that he hadn't run away at all; he had only gone to visit his brother. Joe had heard about the doctor's arrest, and was giving up his freedom to save him. The story has a happy ending: two years later the doctor was dining at a Boston hotel when one of the waiters came to greet him. It was Joe; he had escaped again, as soon as the doctor was safe.

FLIGHT TO THE PROMISED LAND

Harriet Tubman was not the only ex-slave fleeing to Canada because of the second Fugitive Slave Act. As many as three thousand made the move in just the first three months after the act was passed. It's said that in a few black churches in New York State, almost the entire congregation left the country. Some fugitives were carried across the lakes or rivers to Canada by Underground Railroad conductors, in whatever boats they could lay their hands on. Others slipped onto ships when no one was looking, and traveled as stowaways. Many were given free passage by sympathetic ship captains.

One particular ship captain, William Wells Brown, could always be counted on for help. He had been born a slave, and when he was nineteen he and his mother had run away and headed for Canada. They were captured by slave hunters and sent home, and his mother was sold and sent south to New Orleans; mother and son never saw each other again. Later that year William ran away again, and after a hard trip he reached Illinois and set up a ship business. Small wonder that he took pleasure in offering free passage on his boats to escaping slaves! In later years Brown became a novelist, dramatist, historian, and travel writer, as well as a self-taught doctor.

As the system of railroads expanded, some of the slaves escaping on the Underground Railroad were able to travel on *real* trains — not usually as official passengers, but hidden in the baggage and freight, or even with the livestock. The rail companies tended to be sympathetic; some let runaways travel for half-fare, or even for nothing.

THE PENALTIES FOR COURAGE

The more frequent slave escapes became, the more severe became the punishments—by the law or by the mob—for helping the slaves.

In 1844, a shipwright named Jonathan Walker was caught trying to ferry seven slaves to the Bahamas. The unhappy slaves were sent back to their owners; Walker was taken to Florida and fined heavily, displayed in public so that people could throw rotten eggs at him, and branded with an "S S," meaning "slave stealer," burned into his right hand. But branding him turned out to be a mistake; when he returned to the north, he became a popular anti-slavery speaker known as "the man with the branded hand."

Thomas Garrett, a white Quaker in Delaware, was an organizer of the Underground Railroad and a stationmaster who sheltered some 2,700 runaways. He was known for his courageous good humor. When Maryland offered a reward of $10,000 for his capture, he responded that if they would make it $20,000, he would bring *himself* in. A slave owner once threatened him, "If we ever catch you in our part of the world, we'll tar and feather you"; a few weeks later Garrett drove up to the man's door and said, "Here I am," and the embarrassed slave owner could only wave him away: "Go along, Mr. Garrett, no one could do harm to you."

In 1848, Garrett was arrested, tried for his activities, and fined $5,400. He had to auction off his personal possessions to pay the fine. But when the sheriff scolded him, saying, "Thomas, I hope you'll never be caught at this again," the stalwart abolitionist answered, "Friend, I haven't a dollar in the world, but if thee knows a fugitive anywhere on the face of the earth who needs a breakfast, send him to me."

Garrett meant what he said; three years later, when Harriet Tubman arrived on his doorstep with eleven runaways, he gave them all new shoes—and hid them in a secret room behind a wall of shoeboxes.

John Mason was a runaway slave who, like Harriet Tubman, returned to the slave states again and again to rescue others; in all, he helped some 1,300 people to freedom. On one trip he was caught and

A ship arrives at League Island, in Philadelphia, and conductors of the Underground Railroad are waiting with carriages to whisk the escaping slaves away. In the early years of the Railroad, conductors could be quite bold in the northern states, as so few northerners supported slavery. But after the passage of the second Fugitive Slave Act, runaways and their helpers were in grave danger anywhere in the United States.

savagely beaten, and had both his arms broken, before being returned to slavery. But Mason would not give up. A few months later he escaped again, and moved north to Hamilton, Ontario.

Calvin Fairbanks was a minister and a conductor on the Underground Railroad. In his autobiography he described his activities:

I piloted them through the forests, mostly by night; . . . men in women's clothes and women in men's clothes; boys dressed as girls, and girls as boys; on foot or on horseback, in buggies, carriages, common wagons, in and under loads of hay, straw, old furniture, boxes and bags; . . . swimming or wading chin deep; or in boats, or skiffs; on rafts, and often on a pine log. And I never suffered one to be recaptured.

Fairbanks himself was not so lucky; he spent seventeen years in jail for his good deeds.

While many white rescuers were fined or jailed, especially after the second Fugitive Slave Act was passed, they did not suffer as badly as black rescuers or recaptured runaways. *They* were often tortured brutally, and locked into hideous restraining devices. Many were also sold away from their families, to the Deep South, where escape was almost impossible.

The Anti-Slavery Crusade

⋆⇒ ⇐⋆

You're living in the free state of Ohio. One day, as you head home from school, a couple of men grab you and yell, "Pepper Wallace, you little runaway! Wait till your master gets his hands on you!"

"That's not my name!" you cry, struggling in their hands. "And I don't have a master! You have the wrong person!"

"Liar!" shouts one, while the other sneers, "You'll do, you sniveling little brat!"

Suddenly strong hands pull the men off you, and you see that a crowd has collected—an angry crowd. "Filthy slavers!" a man shouts. "It's the devil's work!" says an old woman. As the crowd closes in on the kidnappers, you run away as fast as you can.

With the inspiring public appearances of heroes like Box Brown, the Crafts, and Harriet Tubman, and heartrending newspaper accounts of other daring escapes—and of the misery of those still

(opposite) Frederick Douglass was born into slavery; his mother died when he was eight or nine, and he never knew who his father was. The beatings and starvation he endured as a child made him a fierce abolitionist, as a writer, speaker, activist, and stationmaster for the Underground Railroad. "This struggle may be a moral one; it may be a physical one; or it may be both moral and physical," he said. "But it must be a struggle. Power concedes nothing without a demand."

enslaved—the campaign to abolish slavery completely was growing stronger and stronger in the northern states. Numerous anti-slavery societies were formed, some with junior branches for children. Women held fairs and benefit concerts to raise money for the cause. Funds were collected to help slaves escape, and to help them start building a free life. Pamphlets were handed out in the street, and petitions were sent to Congress. There was a Free Produce movement to boycott southern products—to refuse to buy anything made or grown by slave labor. Orators swayed audiences with powerful speeches about the brutalities of slavery, and linked slave owners to the forces of evil. Abolitionism was more than a political campaign; it was a religious crusade.

Poets too turned their pens to this stirring subject. The Quaker poet John Greenleaf Whittier wrote about slavery many times. He lamented the inhumanity of selling people like animals:

What! mothers from their children riven!
What! God's own image bought and sold!
AMERICANS to market driven,
And bartered as the brute for gold!

He also left no doubt as to who was on God's side, and who was on the devil's:

Speed on the light to those who dwell
In Slavery's land of woe and sin,
And through the blackness of that hell,
Let Heaven's own light break in.

THE ANTI-SLAVERY PRESS

A radical newspaper called *The Liberator* had been founded in 1831 by William Lloyd Garrison, a prominent white abolitionist. In the first issue he declared,

Let Southern oppressors tremble — let their Northern apologists tremble — let all the enemies of the persecuted blacks tremble. I will be as harsh as truth, and as uncompromising as justice. On this subject I do not wish to think, or speak, or write with moderation.... I will not excuse — I will not retreat a single inch — AND I WILL BE HEARD.

Head of "The Liberator."

CHAPTER XIII.

SLAVERY AND ANTI-SLAVERY.

A New Era. — The Modern Anti-slavery Movement. — Garrison and "The Liberator." — His Earnestness and Determination. — Debate on Slavery in Virginia. — The Southampton Insurrection. — Panic at the South. — The Southern Idea of Government. — Slavery met on a New Issue. — The Abolitionists. — The Attempts to suppress Them. — Penal Legislation proposed. — The Resort to Violence. — The Reign of Mobs. — Influence of Slavery on Morals, Manners, Literature, and Commerce.

In 1831 appeared the first sign of a movement which, when contemporaneous passions and prejudices shall have passed away, will be recognized as the beginning and largely the source of a new era in American history. It was a natural consequence of the old slaveholding dispensation that the generation that has passed, or is just passing away, should be made to believe that "Abolitionism" — not slavery — was the sum of all villanies; it was almost inevitable that the next generation should fail to recognize in the influence which governs their time, that very movement of which they know little except that their fathers hated and reviled it. But hated as it was, by those who had eyes enough to see into to-morrow, despised as it was, by the vulgar and the ignorant who have eyes that can hardly see even to-day, the future will discern in this movement the germ of one of those revolutions that overturn dynasties, save nations, and insure continued progress in human affairs.

It was in that year that William Lloyd Garrison, a young printer, from a country town in Massachusetts, established in Boston a newspaper, which he called "The Liberator," to be devoted to the abolition of slavery. He saw, with the vision of a prophet, the long and terrible struggle before him, as he said in the first number of that journal with the eloquence of a sublime pur-

The masthead of William Lloyd Garrison's anti-slavery newspaper was as uncompromising as the editor himself: "I come to break the bonds of the oppressor," it proclaimed, with Jesus as its figurehead. Abolitionists liked to portray the free north as heaven and the slave-owning south as hell, but the comparison made tempers flare on both sides.

Garrison was so unbending that many people considered him a fanatic. The state of Georgia offered $5,000 for his arrest and conviction. On one occasion a pro-slavery mob seized him and tried to hang him, and he was barely rescued in time.

Elijah Lovejoy, a white abolitionist, published a fervent anti-slavery newspaper in Illinois, near the border of the slave state Missouri. Angry mobs demolished three of his printing presses, and in 1837, as he tried to protect a fourth press, Lovejoy was killed.

Another anti-slavery paper was the *North Star*, run by Frederick Douglass. Douglass had been a slave in Maryland; he had taught himself to read and write, and had run away when he was twenty-one. He said little about his escape, and scolded others for talking too much; he pointed out that when they gave away the secrets of the Underground Railroad, they were putting the Railroad in danger. He would only reveal that he had disguised himself as a sailor and used a friend's identification papers. Douglass was such a dignified man, and such a witty and eloquent speaker, that some people found it hard to believe he had really been a slave. He answered their doubts by publishing a book about his experiences, which sold thousands of copies. He was an activist and an organizer, and his house was sometimes used as a station for the Underground Railroad.

Jarmain Wesley Loguen was another ex-slave who published a newspaper, the *Weekly Anglo-African*, and wrote his life story. Loguen was a minister, and with the help of his wife and daughter he ran *two* Underground Railroad stations—one in his home and another in his church. When Loguen became well known, he was outraged to receive a letter from his previous owner. She said she had raised him and his brother and sister as if they were her "own children," and demanded money to make up for his running away. If she didn't get the money, she said, she would sell him to someone else. Despite all that he had accomplished, she still regarded him as her personal property! She was probably as offended by his answer as he was by her letter:

> . . . Woman, did you raise your own children for the market? Did you raise them for the whipping post? Did you raise them to be drove off in a coffle in chains? Where are my poor bleeding brothers and sisters? Can you tell? Who was it that sent them off into sugar and cotton fields, to be kicked, and cuffed, and whipped, and to groan and die? . . .

THE WIDENING GAP BETWEEN NORTH AND SOUTH

In the northern states, the anti-slavery message was loud and clear: in newspapers, in books, in public meetings, and even in the streets. Some people felt that blacks and whites could build a nation together in North America. Others thought the blacks should move to the islands of the Caribbean, and several attempts were made to start colonies there. Yet others believed that whites should help blacks build a modern, democratic, Christian nation on the fertile shores of Africa. In any case, it was generally agreed that slavery was inhuman, barbaric, and simply un-American. The passage of the second Fugitive Slave Act in 1850 made things even worse, for now respected black citizens—craftsmen, publishers, business owners—could be seized from their homes and sent in

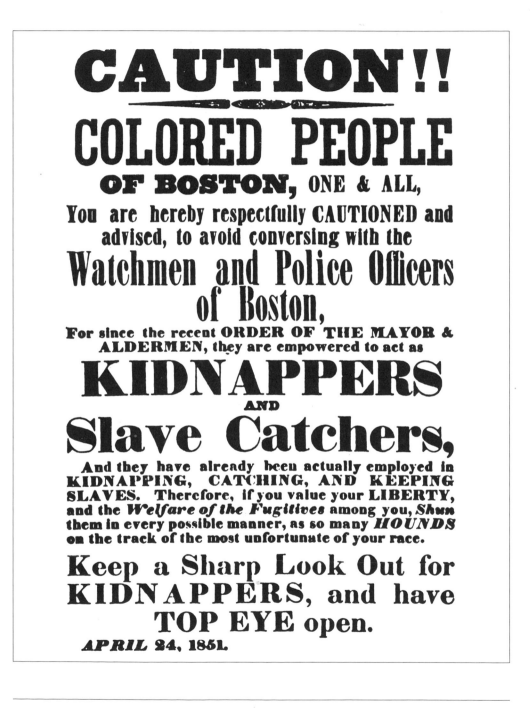

chains back to the cotton fields, and their friends and neighbors could do nothing to help them. Furthermore, the law said that captured blacks had no right to appeal the capture. Their supposed owners simply had to declare that the captured blacks were escaped slaves. Even if the declaration was untrue—even if the blacks had bought their freedom, even if they were *free-born* blacks who were being mistaken for someone else— they had no chance to prove their case. This was an intolerable injustice, and it drew even more northerners to the abolitionist cause.

But in the South the message was barely heard. Slavery was still generally seen as a natural system, in which the "inferior" blacks labored, like horses or oxen, to support the "superior" white civilization that fed them. Southerners insisted that most slave owners were kind, and that most slaves were comfortable and content. In any case, said the pro-slavers, the blacks were too inferior to manage their lives without the help and discipline of a good owner. The northern pressure for abolition was viewed as a political trick to weaken the South, and the accusations of evilness and inhumanity were unspeakable insults. As for the Fugitive Slave Act, it had been passed by the U.S. Congress— as part of a fair bargain—and the northerners who dared to disobey it, to conceal and aid slaves who were somebody else's *legal property*—had to be cheats, thieves, and criminals.

(opposite) Many northern cities had "vigilance committees" working against the slave hunters. They posted notices like this one, kept lists of people suspected of secretly helping kidnappers, and assisted runaways in any way they could.

Blacks being seized by slave hunters. The injustices of the 1850 Fugitive Slave Act
only led to more violence. In 1851, Edward Gorsuch caught his slaves escaping by the
Underground Railroad, and swore he would have either "his property, or breakfast in
hell." As neighbors joined in the fight to protect the fugitives, it became the "Christiana
Riot"; there was gunfire, and Gorsuch was killed. The fugitives escaped, but thirty-one
people were charged with defying the Fugitive Slave Act. William Parker, who had
been hiding the runaways — and was a fugitive himself — barely escaped to Canada,
with the help of Frederick Douglass.

OPEN SEASON FOR THE SLAVE HUNTERS

As the flow of slaves to the north increased, so did the number of slave hunters—and not all of them were as crude and unsophisticated as the ruffians of the dreaded road patrols. There was a New York lawyer who advertised in southern papers, promising to catch and return escaped slaves for the handsome fee of $120. There were "secret agents" in northern cities who took part in abolitionist events, pretending to be sympathizers, as a way to get information about runaways and the Underground Railroad. One slave hunter even posed as an anti-slavery lecturer.

Since their victims weren't allowed to defend themselves, there was no need for the slave hunters to be particular about getting the right person. Some slave hunters didn't bother about owners at all; they just snatched any black they could get, had an accomplice lie about being the owner, and sold their prey at the nearest slave market for a healthy profit.

Two sisters, Rachel and Mary Elizabeth Parker, suffered this fate. They were free blacks working as domestic servants in Pennsylvania. Rachel was seized by two men who broke into the house where she was working and dragged her away. When her employer tried to defend her, he was held off at swordpoint. The next morning Rachel's kidnapper accused her of being the runaway slave of a Mr. Schoolfield, someone she had never heard of:

I told him I was not; he said that I was, and that if I did not say I was he would "cowhide me and salt me, and put me in a dungeon."
I told him I was free, and that I would say nothing but the truth.

Her sister, Mary Elizabeth, had stepped out of doors after clearing the supper table at the house where she worked; she was kidnapped before anyone could help her:

> Afterwards . . . a man told me that I must say that I was Mr. Schoolfield's slave, or he would shoot me, and pulled a "rifle" out of his pocket and showed it to me, and also threatened to whip me.

Both sisters were sold as slaves. But Rachel's employer tried again to rescue her, and was lynched by an angry mob. His death created such public fury that the governor of Pennsylvania intervened, and both women were eventually freed. They were lucky; few of the free blacks who were kidnapped by slave hunters found anyone who would listen to their stories. All too often, the slave hunters' lies were accepted as truth.

But not always.

THE ADVENTURE OF PATRICK SNEAD

In 1853, Patrick Snead was working as a waiter at a hotel at Niagara Falls. Snead had escaped from Georgia and made his way to Canada two years earlier, but he thought no one would recognize him so far north, so he took the chance of working on the American side of the Falls. It was a bad mistake. One day five constables suddenly jumped on him at the hotel, strangling him with his tie and trying to drag him away. When some black waiters came to help him, the constables cried out that Snead was a *murderer*. Snead's friends ignored this shameless lie and managed to wrest him away from the constables and into a ferryboat, and the boat almost reached the safety of the Canadian shore. But the head boatman, hearing the cries to "Stop that murderer!", ordered the boat to come back, and Snead found himself seized again, and borne off in the constables' carriage.

As the carriage dashed away, the head constable asked Snead if he knew anyone in Buffalo, and Snead said he didn't. "Well then," said the constable, "let's go to Buffalo"—for he wanted to deal with his prisoner in a town where there was no one to defend him. But Snead had outwitted his captor:

> We reached Buffalo at ten o'clock at night, when I was put in jail. I told the jailer I wished he would be so good as to tell Lawyer —— to come round to the jail. When the constables saw that, pretending to know no one in Buffalo, I had engaged one of the best lawyers in the place, they were astonished.

When the case came to trial, the lawyer easily got the trumped-up charge of murder thrown out. But the slave hunters had been busy in the meantime, and before Snead could leave the courtroom he faced a new peril: a judge in Georgia had telegraphed that Snead was a runaway and had to be returned under the Fugitive Slave Act. The Buffalo authorities could not refuse to arrest him, but perhaps some kind person chose to dawdle over the paperwork. By the time the new arrest warrant had been sworn, Snead had leapt into a carriage and escaped across the Canadian border—though with a large lawyer's bill in his pocket.

QUEEN OF THE SLAVE HUNTERS

Perhaps the most notorious slave hunter was Patty Cannon, a tall, tough, red-haired woman who ran a kind of Underground Railroad in reverse. She and her gang would kidnap blacks—sometimes by pretending that they were conductors on the Railroad!—and ship them south. Cannon was said to have killed her own husband, and her henchmen were known for their cruelty and torture. Patty Cannon was finally charged with murdering four fugitives (including two children), and she poisoned herself rather than face a public execution. But years later—even after slavery had been abolished—she was still remembered as a monster. As one woman recalled, "We children would hide behind chairs while the big folks told us how evil old Patty Cannon would catch us and sell us to slavers down south."

CROSS-BORDER RAIDS

With big money to be made from slave hunting, even Canada was not an entirely safe haven. Bold slave hunters could easily cross the border and try a little "poaching." Sometimes they made up a story about the runaway stealing something, as an excuse to have their prey sent back to the United States (though Canadian courts had heard these stories too often, and usually gave the fugitive the benefit of the doubt).

In 1830, an ex-slave named Andrew was working as a farmhand for the Baby family in Sandwich (now part of Windsor, Ontario). Andrew's previous owner tracked him down and tried to buy him back for $2,000, claiming that Andrew had stolen a horse. Andrew insisted that he was innocent, and Mr. Baby believed him, and refused to consider the offer. The owner then returned to the United States, and came back with five kidnappers, timing their arrival for an hour when the Baby family would be at church. But Mr. Baby had stayed home that day, and he and his neighbors fought off the attackers. Then they collected enough money to send Andrew to Toronto, farther away from the dangers of the border.

Even Toronto was not always safe. In 1840 a local newspaper, the *Toronto Patriot*, reported that two men, "Irishmen we believe by birth but Yankeefied by habit," had tried to kidnap a black man at knifepoint, claiming that he was their slave. The paper concluded by reassuring its readers, somewhat smugly:

> The parties after being suitably reprimanded . . . for the brutal and cowardly practice of carrying bowie knives, and made aware that under Monarchical Institutions and British Laws, there existed no excuse for wearing such weapons, were severally fined Five Pounds, and held to bail for their future good conduct.

Then again, sometimes it was Canadians who did the "snatching." In 1840 a party of tourists from the southern United States were dining in a Canadian resort near Niagara Falls, when some forty or fifty black militiamen surrounded the hotel and tried to liberate the tourists' two black female slaves. The gallant attempt failed, but apparently the militiamen were not punished for their impromptu campaign.

In 1858, Elijah Leonard, once mayor of London, Ontario, noticed an arrogant white American at the town's railway station, with a young black boy. Realizing that the child had been kidnapped, and was being taken south to be a slave, Leonard confided in Anderson Diddrick, a local black who also happened to be present. By this time the train was leaving for Detroit, but Leonard knew it would stop in Chatham, Ontario.

I asked [Diddrick] if he knew anyone in Chatham. "Yes, several." "Would they take this boy away from this man?" "Yes, they would," but he added he had no money to telegraph. I gave him some, and he immediately wired the state of affairs. . . .

Isabella Baumfree worked as a free domestic servant until she was forty-six, when she found herself called by God to speak out against slavery. Carrying a bundle of clothes and a basket of food, she traveled across the United States, spreading the word. She chose a new name, Sojourner Truth, "because I was to travel up and down the land [and] because I was to declare the truth to the people." Despite her plain dress and her lack of education, she was a powerful and persuasive presence, and a good friend of Frederick Douglass.

When the train reached Chatham, it was stormed by almost a hundred black men and women armed with clubs, and the boy was handed over without argument. As Elijah Leonard noted, "Mr. Kidnapper was very glad to get off with a whole skin. . . ."

A COUNTRY STRAINED TO BREAKING

As abolitionists spread the word that God was on their side, and that slavery was an invention straight from hell, there were more and more riots to rescue runaways from slave hunters, courthouses, and jails. As slave owners saw their "property" escaping and their whole way of life endangered, they turned more and more to violence to take back their slaves and punish those who helped them. The most extreme pro-slavers—called "fire eaters"—had made up their minds to split the country in half rather than lose their slaves. On both sides there was bloodshed and there was death, and with so much anger and bitterness there seemed to be no way back. The country that called itself "the United States" was hopelessly divided. How much longer could it hold together?

Fiery Words and Fiery Deeds

·✦·⇌ ⇋·✦·

"This is God's curse on slavery! — a bitter, bitter, most accursed thing! a curse to the master and a curse to the slave! . . . It is a sin to hold a slave under laws like ours, — I always felt it was. . . ."

Despite all the speeches, pamphlets, and autobiographies penned in the abolition campaign, probably the writing that did the most to end American slavery was a novel published in 1852. In a lively, colorful book called *Uncle Tom's Cabin*, Harriet Beecher Stowe combined details from a number of true-life adventures and tragedies to create a heartrending tale of life under slavery.

(opposite) Harriet Beecher Stowe, the author of Uncle Tom's Cabin, *grew up in an atmosphere of religious piety and humanitarian reform; her father was a Congregational minister, her sister a teacher. Her husband was a professor of languages and religion, and their home was a station on the Underground Railroad. Stowe herself wrote religious articles and poems, and supported reform campaigns for various causes, such as temperance (against drinking) and women's suffrage (votes for women). Her lively writing and sense of humor won her many readers. Of herself, she once said she was "about as thin and dry as a pinch of snuff; never very much to look at in my best days, and looking like a used-up article now."*

135,000 SETS, 270,000 VOLUMES SOLD.

UNCLE TOM'S CABIN

FOR SALE HERE.

AN EDITION FOR THE MILLION, COMPLETE IN 1 Vol., PRICE 37 1-2 CENTS.
"   "   IN GERMAN, IN 1 Vol., PRICE 50 CENTS.
"   "   IN 2 Vols,. CLOTH, 6 PLATES, PRICE $1.50.
SUPERB ILLUSTRATED EDITION, IN 1 Vol., WITH 153 ENGRAVINGS,
PRICES FROM $2.50 TO $5.00.

The Greatest Book of the Age.

An advertisement for Uncle Tom's Cabin. *Only the Bible was selling more copies.*

The story opens in Kentucky, where Uncle Tom and his wife and children work on the estate of the Shelby family. Although they are slaves, they enjoy a cheerful, cozy life, and Uncle Tom has been promised many times that he will be given his freedom. He is so honest and trustworthy that he can be sent anywhere, with any money or property, and he will always come back. He believes it would be dishonorable to run away from his kind master and his loving family.

Mrs. Shelby's young maid, Eliza Harris, is also happy with her life as a slave; her husband, George, works nearby and visits her often, and she adores her little boy, Harry.

But terrible things are happening. Mr. Shelby owes money to a ruthless slave trader, and can avoid financial ruin only by selling Uncle Tom and little Harry. And George is moved from his good job to hard labor, and is told to forget Eliza and marry someone else. George runs

An illustration from the book: Eliza tells Uncle Tom that he has been sold and that she is running away to save her child. Harriet Beecher Stowe originally planned Uncle Tom's Cabin *to be three or four chapters in an abolitionist newspaper, but readers demanded more and more episodes, and the story grew into a lengthy novel.*

away and heads for Canada, promising to find money to buy Eliza. Then Eliza runs away too, trying to get little Harry to safety. After many close calls, Eliza and George and Harry reach Canada and find a new life.

But not Uncle Tom. Instead of running away, he deliberately lets himself be sold, to help the Shelbys. He asks only that they try to save up money to buy him back. Then he says goodbye to his family and is shipped south in shackles and handcuffs. He is bought by the St. Clare

Many episodes in Uncle Tom's Cabin *were based on real events. One dramatic scene shows Eliza fleeing the slave catchers by carrying little Harry across the spring ice breaking up on the Ohio River:*

> *The huge green fragment of ice . . . pitched and creaked as her weight came on it, but she staid there not a moment. With wild cries and desperate energy she leaped to another and still another cake; — tumbling — leaping — slipping — springing upwards again! Her shoes are gone — her stockings cut from her feet — while blood marked every step. . . .*

A real-life Eliza Harris had escaped in exactly this way, carrying her young daughter; across the river she was guided to the home of a Quaker couple, Levi and Catherine Coffin, and the Underground Railroad helped her reach Canada.

family, and becomes devoted to their little blond daughter, Eva. He is as faithful to the St. Clares as he was to the Shelbys, and again he is promised that *soon* he will have his freedom.

But tragedy strikes again. Little Eva wastes away and dies, and her father is killed in a fight, and suddenly Uncle Tom finds himself sold to a

The character of Uncle Tom himself was based partly on Josiah Henson. Henson was a loyal slave who served his owner faithfully and was promised his freedom for

$450. He became a Methodist preacher and worked hard to earn the money, but as soon as he had enough, his owner changed the price to $1,000. Despite being cheated, Henson remained loyal — until he learned that his owner was secretly planning to sell him away from his wife and four children. Unlike Uncle Tom, Josiah Henson escaped to Canada with his family, in 1830. In 1849 he wrote the story of his life. From this book, and from their personal conversations, Harriet Beecher Stowe drew many details for her novel.

vicious slave owner named Simon Legree. Legree despises Uncle Tom's saintliness, and resolves to corrupt him by turning him into an overseer. When Uncle Tom is ordered to whip a slave woman, he absolutely refuses, and he is savagely flogged as punishment. As he lies broken and bleeding, the son of the Shelby family arrives with the money to buy Uncle Tom's freedom; he will take Uncle Tom back to his loving wife and

Runaways arrive at the home of Levi and Catherine Coffin. The Coffin family were prominent in the Underground Railroad. It may have been Levi's cousin Vestal who first organized the Railroad, around 1819. The home of Levi and Catherine was an important station on the intersection of three different escape routes — it has been called the Railroad's "Grand Central Station." The Quaker storekeeper was also very successful at raising money to keep the operation running. After a trip to Canada in 1844, to see how the escapees were faring in their new home, he began collecting money for them as well.

children. Too late—Uncle Tom is dying. With his last words he forgives the evil Simon Legree: "He an't done me no real harm,—only opened the gate of the kingdom [of heaven] for me; that's all."

There was hardly a dry eye from Maine to Wisconsin. The book sold three hundred thousand copies in its first year, as printing presses ran day and night to keep up with the demand. The story was turned into a popular play. The book was published all over Europe and translated into twenty-three languages, and the author became an international celebrity. Simply owning the book was a criminal offense in the slave-owning states.

No matter how indifferent people were to "politics"—no matter how little they cared about pamphlets and petitions and public meetings—they couldn't resist the emotional appeal of the novel. There was poor Uncle Tom, whose features had

an expression of grave and steady good sense, united with much kindliness and benevolence. There was something about his whole air self-respecting and dignified, yet united with a confiding and humble simplicity.

There was George's scathing description of slave owners:

". . . they get along so easy in the world, and have it all their own way; and poor, honest, faithful Christians . . . are lying in the very dust under their feet. They buy 'em and sell 'em, and make trade of their heart's blood, and groans and tears, —and God *lets* them."

There was Simon Legree's cruelty to slaves:

> "I used to, when I fust begun, have considerable trouble . . . doctorin' on 'em up when they's sick, and givin' on 'em clothes and blankets, and what not. . . . Law, 'twasn't no sort o' use; I lost money on 'em, and 'twas heaps o' trouble. Now, you see, I just put 'em straight through, sick or well. When one nigger's dead, I buy another; and I find it comes cheaper and easier, every way."

Finally, there was young Mr. Shelby's declaration as he told all his slaves that they were free:

> "It was on [Uncle Tom's] grave, my friends, that I resolved, before God, that I would never own another slave. . . ."

BLOOD FOR BLOOD

Just four years after *Uncle Tom's Cabin* was published, the feud between proslavers and abolitionists erupted in a pair of violent raids. The town of Lawrence, Kansas—near the border of the slave state Missouri—was a major stop on the Underground Railroad, and an abolitionist center. In 1856, a mob of some eight hundred proslavers swept down on the town, robbed the inhabitants of money and jewelry, and burned many of the buildings. In revenge, a group led by John Brown—a passionate abolitionist who hoped to make Kansas a refuge for runaways, like Canada— carried out a nighttime raid in which five pro-slavers were dragged from their beds and hacked to death. The result was a "guerrilla war" along the

Kansas–Missouri border, as pro-slavers fought to keep fugitives from slipping across to freedom.

THE DRED SCOTT CASE

The next year, a scandalous court case brought new fire to the anti-slavery campaign. Dred Scott had been born a slave, but had accompanied his owner into free states, and had lived and married there. After his owner died, Scott sued for freedom, saying that by living in free territories he had gained his liberty. At first he won, but the ruling was appealed and finally went to the Supreme Court. The judges disagreed vehemently among themselves, but Scott lost the case. It was proclaimed that a person descended from slaves had *no rights as a citizen*, and therefore no right to sue in court. Abolitionists were shocked by the shameful decision, and it made them even more determined to put an end to such injustice.

THE HARPERS FERRY RAID

In 1859 — two years after Dred Scott lost his freedom — a group of abolitionists, both black and white, decided to take matters into their own hands. Their leader — John Brown again — had come up with a dangerous and wildly ambitious plan. His idea was that a unit of skilled commando fighters should install themselves in a stronghold in the Virginia mountains, and start raiding the surrounding plantations, freeing as many slaves as possible. Some of the slaves would join this "army," and others would be funneled into Canada, using routes and hiding places suggested by Harriet Tubman. Brown did most of his organizing in Chatham, where Tubman was living, and even hoped to raise a small army of Canadians to help get the fugitives across the border. When his army was large enough, Brown promised, it would march south and take over the slave states entirely.

The plan was breathtaking; the reality was a disaster. Brown's first step was to attack a government arsenal at Harpers Ferry, Virginia, to steal a hoard of guns and ammunition for his planned army. But government troops arrived and overpowered the raiders, and ten of them died—including two of John Brown's sons. Brown was hanged for treason, conspiracy, and murder in December 1859. To opponents of slavery on both sides of the border, he remained a hero and a martyr who had laid down his life in the cause of freedom.

UNITED NO MORE

In 1854, a new political party had been formed in the United States. It was called the Republican Party, and it opposed slavery in any new territories; it also denounced the Dred Scott decision. Naturally, the southern states regarded the new party with deep mistrust. But in the North the Republicans gained support rapidly, and in 1860 they chose a little-known lawyer as their new leader. His name was Abraham Lincoln.

(opposite) Although John Brown was involved in some bloody deeds, and was regarded by many as a madman, to others he was a great hero. On his way to be hanged he stopped to kiss a black baby. Before he died he bravely declared that if he had to die to bring justice, "and mingle my blood further with the blood of my children and with the blood of millions in this slave country whose rights are disregarded by wicked, cruel and unjust enactments, I say let it be done."

Born in 1809, Lincoln had grown up in poverty, and was mainly self-taught. While working on his education, he had held many jobs and traveled to many places. He continued to travel after he entered politics, but sometimes he didn't say who he was. A slave named Mingo White reported that Lincoln spent the night and watched with a sharp eye to see how the slaves were treated:

> When he got back up North he writ Old Master a letter and told him he was going to have to free his slaves, that everybody was going to, that the North was going to see to it. He also told him . . . to go in the room he slept in and look on the bedstead at the head and he'd see where he'd writ his name. Sure enough, there was his name: A. Lincoln.

Lincoln disliked slavery, considering it evil and unjust, and he did not want any new slaveholding territories created. Yet he did not believe that slavery should simply be abolished, because he knew the southern states would utterly reject a total ban on slavery, and above all he wanted to preserve the country intact. Two years before, he had made careful reference to the dilemma in a political speech:

> A house divided against itself cannot stand. I believe this government cannot endure permanently half slave and half free. I do not expect the Union to be dissolved—I do not expect the house to fall—but I do expect it will cease to be divided. It will become all one thing, or all the other.

But which of the two would the country become — all free, or all slaveholding? And who would make the decision?

In 1860, Abraham Lincoln was elected president of the United States. The southern states realized that, sooner or later, slavery would be outlawed, whether they agreed or not. One by one, they began to secede — that is, they withdrew from the United States and joined together to create a country of their own, with Jefferson Davis as president. The deals and compromises had failed, and the "house" of the United States had fallen after all. In its place were two nations: the free Union in the North, and the slaveholding Confederacy in the South.

New Life, New Land

-<>==() (==<>-

You sit on the boat, watching the distant shore come nearer. How strange it seems to be leaving the United States! But you never felt safe there after the last Fugitive Slave Act was passed; the slave hunters were always prowling about, with their shackles and their shameless lies.

You remember the stories you've heard about Canada—how it's frozen for half the year, how the wolves and bears carry away small children. What if you can't get a job? What if you can't find a place to live? You have hardly any money, and no friends in Canada—you don't know anything about this place—what's going to happen to you now?

While the union of the northern and southern states was collapsing, the British territories north of the U.S. border were moving toward "confederation"—joining together to make a new country. The colonies were thriving, with spreading farmlands and growing towns and cities. Upper and Lower Canada (Ontario and Quebec) had been renamed Canada West and Canada East, and combined into the Province of Canada. But there were political problems that a wider union might solve. There was also a fear that the colonies might be invaded by Americans—it had happened in the War of 1812, and would happen again in 1866. As railroad tracks spanned the country and distances

A family of ex-slaves in Ontario in the 1850s. Although blacks faced prejudice in Canada, they also found freedom and legal rights. Henry Williamson, who escaped from Maryland to Hamilton, Ontario, said, "I feel as if a weight were off me. Nothing would induce me to go back. . . . I would rather be wholly poor, and be free, than to have all I could wish and be a slave."

seemed shorter, people started dreaming of a strong, independent land that would reach from sea to sea.

By this time, black communities were established in many Canadian towns and cities, as well as farming areas. Some of their white neighbors were truly helpful and sympathetic; some were openly racist; many were indifferent, willing to tolerate the blacks, but not to mix too closely with them.

In the 1850s and 1860s, a number of whites and ex-slaves living in Ontario were asked for their opinion of how the blacks were getting on. Most said that racial prejudice was a problem, but that it didn't prevent blacks from building a good life. Many immigrants from Britain and Europe had never known black people before, and were suspicious of what was unfamiliar. White immigrants from the United States sometimes brought racist attitudes with them. For that matter, some ex-slaves remained wary and resentful of whites. "Some of our people are very jealous of the white people," admitted Henry Williamson, of Hamilton. "If they approach them with the best intentions in the world, they are suspicious, and will not communicate any thing, even if it were to their own benefit." With tension and distrust on both sides, there was bound to be conflict.

Economic pressure made matters worse. With so many people struggling to feed their families and build a new life, there were times when whites objected to black competition. Some fugitives were refused the chance to buy land; others were pushed off land they had already worked to clear, on the excuse of legal technicalities. And there were more aggressive incidents. A Mr. Sinclair of Chatham noted that there was one township where no blacks had been allowed to settle: "One man has tried to build a house there, but as fast as he built it in the day time, the white people would pull it down at night." Mr. McCullum, the white principal of Hamilton High School, noted that white laborers had been charging a good price for sawing wood; when black workers arrived, desperate for jobs, they charged less. "What did the white people do? They raised a mob, went one night and burned every shanty that belonged to a colored person, and drove them off entirely."

Most ex-slaves had little education, and that made their position even more difficult. Benjamin Miller, of London, Ontario, pointed out:

We that begin here illiterate men, have to go against wind and tide. We have a learned, enterprising people to contend with; we have a colder climate than we have been used to . . . ; we have our own ignorance and poverty to contend with. It takes a smart man to do all that: but many do it. . . .

Another black, George Sunter, expressed his resentment in a bitterly eloquent letter to a Brantford, Ontario, newspaper:

You reproach us with our poverty; we bring no wealth to the province, forsooth! We bring what is better, a test of your morals, an occasion for that *justice*, the meaning of which you have well nigh forgot, and for a reinstatement of those principles of *liberty* which you would betray and banish.

EQUAL IN THE LAW

But while black settlers might be treated as inferior by some of their neighbors, in the eyes of the law they were equal, at least in principle. They could own land, they could vote, they could send their children to school and college, and they had the same rights, in court, as any white. If prejudice took the form of crime, they could have their persecutors sent to jail — which is what happened to the men who burned the blacks' homes in the wood-sawing dispute.

A Mrs. Brown of St. Catharines, Ontario, complained of prejudice — "When I was at home, I could go anywhere; but here, my goodness! you get an insult on every side" — but added that she stayed in Canada because "the colored people have their rights before the law." A Mr. Simpson of Toronto agreed: "The law is the only thing that sustains us in this country." William Grose of St. Catharines explained how different it felt to have "the rights and privileges of any other man":

> When in the United States, if a white man spoke to me, I would
> feel frightened . . . ; but now . . . I can look him right in the eyes —
> if he were to insult me, I could give him an answer. . . . Now I feel
> like a man, and I wish to God that all my fellow creatures could
> feel the same freedom. . . .

STARTING FROM SCRATCH

But while legal rights are valuable, you can't eat them, and you can't wear them. So how do you go about building a new life, in a cold, harsh country, when all you have is the clothes on your back? That was the question Josiah Henson (of *Uncle Tom* fame) faced when he and his family crossed the border in 1830. After his first wild rejoicing — hugging the

Most families arrived with nothing, and lived in poverty for the first few years.

ground with such "riotous exultation" that bystanders thought he must be having a fit—Henson visited a local landowner and asked if he could work in exchange for a place to live.

> [The owner] said yes, and led the way to an old two story sort of shanty, into the lower story of which the pigs had broken, and apparently made it their resting-place for some time. Still, it was a house, and I forthwith expelled the pigs, and set about cleaning it. . . .

Henson worked till midnight, digging out the filth and cleaning the floor, and made beds by piling straw into log bins in the corners. For three years the family lived there, gradually buying some pigs, a cow, and a horse. Meanwhile Henson learned to read, began preaching in the local church, and had the great satisfaction of seeing his children go to school.

As his own life improved, Henson was troubled to see other black refugees working as hired laborers instead of using their new freedom. He and some friends decided to work together

> upon wild lands which we could call our own; and where every tree which we felled, and every bushel of corn we raised, would be for ourselves . . . where we would colonize and raise our own crops, and eat our own bread and be, in short, our own masters.

The settlement they created became home to many of the blacks fleeing across the border—including some brought over by Henson himself, on the Underground Railroad.

LENDING A HELPING HAND

In the 1840s, Josiah Henson took part in a more ambitious project called the Dawn Institute. This was a black community near Dresden, Ontario, that had a school and a commercial sawmill, and gave immigrants a basic education and some industrial training.

A similar community, the Wilberforce settlement, had been created north of London, Ontario, in 1829. A group of ex-slaves from Cincinnati and Boston had undertaken the backbreaking job of clearing the forest, and had built a settlement with a large herd of cattle, homes, two schools, and eventually a small church.

In the 1850s, the Refugee Home Society bought land in Sandwich (Windsor) and elsewhere, gave immigrants basic schooling, and helped them set up fruit farms.

All these projects, and others like them, had similar aims; they collected money (mainly from the United States) and bought large blocks of land, and then resold small parcels of the land on easy terms to black immigrants. As well, they gave settlers enough education and practical knowledge to get started. The settlements had limited success; life was hard, and families drifted away to towns. There were management problems, too, because often the people running the settlements had no experience in such projects. Still, these free black settlements provided a much-needed home for fugitives, and encouraged other slaves to make the desperate run for freedom.

THE ELGIN SETTLEMENT

One settlement, however, was a dramatic success. In 1849, an Irish-born minister named William King persuaded the Presbyterian Church to create a black community near Chatham, Ontario. Edwin Larwill, an influential local merchant, fiercely opposed the plan, telling the townspeople that blacks were inferior and irresponsible and that the town would suffer from their presence. Larwill organized a vigilante committee, and King was warned that his life was in danger, but he refused to back down. When he made a speech in Chatham to defend his plan, a dozen armed black men stood guard around him. Only one other white man, Archibald McKellar, stood beside King as he faced the booing crowd.

In 1854, Edwin Larwill — the enemy of the Elgin settlement — became a Member of Parliament. But as property owners, the Elgin settlers had the right to vote, and in the election of 1856 they had the pleasure of casting their ballots and wiping Larwill out of politics. The new M.P. was Archibald McKellar, the man who had stood beside King when the settlement was first planned.

The settlement received money from Presbyterian churches, but it was the settlers who did all the work. Starting in the winter of 1849, each family built a sturdy log house with a picket fence; together they cleared the land, opened roads, and dug drainage ditches. When spring came, they planted vegetables and flowers, and started crops of hemp, wheat, and tobacco. To earn money for supplies, they worked on construction of the nearby railway.

By summer they had built a small post office, and a school that also served as a church. Within a few years they had plenty of farm animals, a brickyard, two mills, and a country store. Teachers from Knox Presbyterian College in Toronto included Latin and Greek in the school program, and white students flocked to enroll. Elgin had the best school for miles around, and its black graduates would become doctors, teachers, lawyers, and public officials.

The Elgin settlement was important for the good start it gave to many ex-slaves and their children. But it was also important because it proved that the Larwills of the world were wrong. Given half a chance, the people fleeing slavery would be responsible, hardworking, successful citizens—and their children would take their places in every level of life.

SEPARATING THE CHILDREN

Unfortunately, Elgin was an exception; few black children went to good schools. At first, they had the legal right to go to public schools—and many teachers were happy to teach them. But often the white parents refused to let their children sit beside blacks; either the black children weren't allowed in, or they were put at the back of the class and ridiculed. Many black parents preferred to set up their own schools rather than put their children through such humiliation.

In 1850, Canada West (now Ontario) authorized separate schools for blacks, and many communities took that to mean that black children *had* to go to black schools, whether they wanted to or not. But these schools were usually much worse than the ones for white children, with poor facilities, little equipment, and inexperienced teachers. In the Maritimes too, most black children went to separate schools that were far below the standards of white education.

SEGREGATION IN THE HOUSE OF GOD

Many ex-slaves were deeply religious—with their hard lives, they had had little to keep them going but their faith in God, and their hope for happiness in heaven. But when they came to Canada, they found that they were unwelcome in some churches. Prejudice was part of the reason, but the main objection was to their style of worship: they spoke differently, sang different hymns, and were more enthusiastic than most white worshipers. So perhaps both sides were more comfortable when the fugitives began to build their own churches—often with donations from white congregations. Still, it was ironic that the churches that had worked so zealously to convert slaves to Christianity could not now make them welcome.

SETTLING IN

When runaways escaped into Canada, they became free—but with freedom came new responsibilities. Slaves, after all, received their homes and clothes and meals from their owners. The homes might be rickety shacks, the clothes might be rags, the meals might be scraps—but they were provided. Imagine how it must have felt to arrive in Canada—uneducated, with empty pockets, and far from family and friends—and to realize that nobody had to give you *anything*.

Fortunately, help was at hand. There were refugee associations, both black and white, that collected money in Canada and the United States. There were the black settlements, where a family could buy a little land and keep food on the table while they learned a trade. Some fugitives were already skilled—as barbers, masons, or shoemakers.

When white parents objected to black children in the public schools, money was set aside for separate black schools — but the schools were usually much worse than the ones for whites. Churches and religious societies stepped in and built "mission schools" to help black children get a good start in life.

Some turned their slave experience into jobs as cooks, maids, or hairdressers. Others hired out as unskilled help, and learned on the job. Sooner or later, most of them moved to cities and towns.

By the 1850s there were substantial black communities in Hamilton, St. Catharines, Chatham, London, Windsor, and many other Ontario centers. In Toronto there were about a thousand blacks, working in all sorts of trades:

> Levi Lightfoot owned a shoe-repair shop; his two sons later became a dentist and a doctor. Philip Judah owned a tobacco shop as well as a large fruit market. . . . The first ice company in Toronto was owned by a Black who cut ice [to keep food cold] from the mill ponds beyond Bloor Street.

(left) William Hall was born in Nova Scotia in 1828, and went to sea when he was twelve. He sailed with the Royal Navy and served in the Crimean War. In 1857 he helped relieve a British garrison besieged in Lucknow, India, and won the Victoria Cross for his outstanding bravery.

(right) Delos Rogest Davis was born in the slave state of Maryland, but got to Canada when he was four. He worked his way up from sailor and millworker to teacher, and studied law, and in 1884 a special act was passed to let him become Canada's first black lawyer. In 1910, Davis was named a K.C. — "King's Counsel" — a high honor. He was the first black K.C. in the British Empire.

(right) When gold was discovered in British Columbia, starting in the 1850s, blacks joined the flood of prospectors hoping to make their fortunes. Samuel Booth found a gold nugget the size of an egg. He is shown here in his Mason's regalia. (The Masons are a charity organization with secret signs and rituals.) Other blacks moved to the gold-rush towns and set up stores, restaurants, and barbershops where the miners could spend their new wealth.

(left) Elijah McCoy was born in Canada; his parents had escaped from Kentucky by the Underground Railroad. McCoy became a mechanical engineer, and after Emancipation he went to the United States to be a railroad mechanic and inventor. One of his inventions was an automatic oiler that meant steam engines didn't have to be stopped and restarted every time they needed oil. It was used on locomotives, factory engines, and transatlantic steamboats, and was so superior that it became known as "the real McCoy."

Toronto was a center of abolitionist feeling. One reason was George Brown, a reformist politician and founder of the *Globe* (now the *Globe and Mail*). Brown was strongly anti-racist, and his newspaper was quick to denounce discrimination. When he was running for Parliament, certain people promised to vote for him if he would segregate the schools and put a special tax on black immigrants. "There were 150 men degraded enough to sign such a paper and send it to me," said Brown with disgust. There was no tax, and Toronto's schools remained open to all.

In Sandwich (Windsor, Ontario), Henry Bibb—a noted orator and

a leader of the Refugee Home Society—published the *Voice of the Fugitive*, a newspaper that helped immigrants find work and settle into their new homes; it also took a strong

Henry Bibb, publisher of the Voice of the Fugitive *and founder of the Refugee Home Society. In 1852, Bibb was accused of keeping some of the money he raised for settlers; in 1853, his printing office was burned down, perhaps by an arsonist; in 1854, he died. He was just thirty-nine.*

Strong-willed and independent, Mary Ann Shadd believed firmly in education, and started teaching school in the United States when she was just sixteen. She moved to Canada in 1850, when the second Fugitive Slave Act was passed, and published a booklet telling American blacks the truth about Canada's opportunities, and urging them to move north. In 1853, she became editor and business manager of a newspaper, the Provincial Freeman — *probably the first woman in Canada to hold such a position.*

stand against racial prejudice. Bibb had escaped slavery in Kentucky, and had lectured for ten years as a dedicated abolitionist before retreating to Canada when the second Fugitive Slave Act was passed.

Another black newspaper, the *Provincial Freeman*, was equally opposed to racism, but said there was too much fundraising going on. The paper suggested that black settlers didn't need so many handouts, that the constant "begging" by fundraisers was degrading, and that much of the money raised never even reached the people it was meant for. The paper also objected to black settlements like Dawn and Elgin, arguing

In the days before household appliances, few women were in the public eye. Most labored over housework and raised children; many earned a little money as servants, seamstresses, or washerwomen; some helped out in their husbands' businesses.

Only a few times in their lives did they dress up in their best finery and go off for a portrait photograph. We don't know these women's names, or where they came from. All we know is what we can read in their faces.

that blacks would never find their place in Canada until they were fully integrated—in towns, in churches, and in schools. The *Provincial Freeman* had been founded by Samuel Ringgold Ward, a celebrated lecturer and preacher who had operated two newspapers in the United States before taking refuge in Canada. But it was run by Mary Ann Shadd, the first black woman to head a North American newspaper.

The first military unit ever formed in British Columbia was the Victoria Pioneer Rifle Corps. This black unit, known as the African Rifles, was put together in 1860 to defend Canada against the Americans, and lasted until 1866. The soldiers worked without pay, built their own drill hall, and ordered uniforms all the way from England, but for a long time the only guns they could get were "archaic flintlocks, borrowed from the Hudson's Bay Company, which were little better than broomsticks." Blacks also formed the first police force in Victoria, the capital of the colony, but within weeks they were replaced by whites because of racist protest and threats of violence.

A FRIEND IN THE WEST

On the West Coast the blacks found a powerful ally. James Douglas, governor of British Columbia, had been born in South America, of a mother who was partly black; his wife's mother was a native Canadian. Although California was a free state, in the 1850s a number of laws were passed to limit the civil rights of blacks. With Douglas's encouragement, hundreds moved north. Unlike many of the runaways arriving in eastern Canada, these were free people, with education and skills, and often money as well. Although they faced some prejudice, they were accepted in the schools and churches, and enjoyed more equality than most blacks in Canada.

BUILDING A COMMUNITY

And so the American blacks settled in. They saved money, bought houses, and sent their children to school; they made friends, built churches, and took part in local politics. They formed musical groups, debating societies, and literary associations; they organized refugee societies to help new arrivals, and benevolent associations to assist people who were too sick to work. And every year they celebrated Emancipation Day — the anniversary of the 1833 act that had abolished slavery throughout the British Empire — with parades, church services, banquets, speeches, and football games.

Despite these signs of contentment, though, many of them still thought of the United States as their home, and looked forward to the day when they would be able to return. They watched with deep concern as tensions grew between the northern and southern states, until the country finally split in two in 1860. What would happen next?

Free at Last!

⤙═ ⊂═ ⤚

War? How can there be a war? You think of families you knew back south—the Haydens, with two of their sons living up in Wisconsin; Mrs. Turner, always talking about her dear sister up in Maine. How can there be a war when half the soldiers have loved ones on the "enemy" side? And for the slaves, which side is the enemy? The North promises them freedom, but the South is their home, their lives, their families.

How can a country have a war with itself? And when the war is over, will anything be left?

(opposite) For President Lincoln, who was known for his honesty and strong moral principles, slavery was a troubling dilemma. He opposed the idea that one person could own another; but the southern states had been guaranteed the right to keep slaves, and he felt it would be wrong to break that promise. Yet he admitted that the ideas of slavery and freedom were bound to collide some day. "They are like two wild beasts in sight of each other, but chained and apart," he said. "Some day these deadly antagonists will . . . break their bonds, and then the question will be settled."

It would be settled in April 1865, when the South lost the war against the North and the slaves were freed. Five days later, Lincoln was fatally shot by John Wilkes Booth, a deranged actor who shouted, "Sic semper tyrannis! [Thus to all tyranny!] The South is avenged!"

When Abraham Lincoln was elected president and seven of the southern states broke away to form their own country, at first people hoped that a war could be avoided. Perhaps they could find a compromise that would bring the United States back together. Or perhaps the two countries—the Union in the North and the Confederacy in the South—could live side by side in peace.

Lincoln rejected the southern secession, saying that the Union could not be broken up, but he also promised that the North would not be the first to attack. But with the country splitting in two, and with so much anger and suspicion on both sides, violence was inevitable.

THE WAR BETWEEN THE STATES

In the harbor of Charleston, South Carolina—a southern state—there were three forts manned by Union soldiers. The South demanded their surrender. The North responded by moving all the men to the strongest one, Fort Sumter. The South seized the other two forts, and an arsenal full of weapons, and cut off supplies to Fort Sumter, again demanding its surrender. When the North again refused, and ordered the navy to take supplies to the besieged fort, the South attacked.

Lincoln called up the militia—a civilian army used for emergencies—and made other preparations for war. His actions drove four more southern states to secede. Only four slave states still remained in the Union—all right on the Union border.

Although the Fort Sumter incident was finally resolved without bloodshed, there was now no going back. The once-united states were at war.

It was not an even match. The Union had more money, more than twice the population, and far more factories to make weapons and war goods. It had a larger navy, so it could attack the Confederacy along the rivers and the seacoast, and could also blockade the coast, stopping any

When the Civil War began, blacks were not allowed into the Union army or the Confederate army. After Emancipation they were free to fight on the Union side, and more than 180,000 signed up. A third of them were dead or missing by the time the war was over. The Confederate army never allowed black soldiers, but used slaves as laborers and officers' servants.

A Union soldier reads the Emancipation Proclamation to blacks in the South. But until the South was defeated, the proclamation was just a piece of paper.

foreign ships that tried to bring supplies to the South. The South had hoped for help from Britain, because British manufacturers depended on cheap cotton from the slave plantations, but Britain decided not to take sides. The South was alone.

It was a bloody and terribly bitter war. Many families were split, with some relatives fighting on one side and some on the other. Free blacks rushed to join the Union army, to help put an end to slavery once and for all. Black slaves in the South were torn between their loyalty to the families and states they had served for years, and their yearning to be free: many stayed in the South, but some slipped away to join the Union army.

Now that North and South were at war anyway, the abolitionists said President Lincoln should proclaim an end to slavery throughout the states. At first Lincoln refused. He believed that emancipation (freedom) should come gradually. Also, he didn't want to drive away the four slave states that were still in the Union. But in 1862 he chose a compromise: he declared that slaves in the *rebel* southern states were free, but he did nothing for the slaves in the loyal border states. This "Emancipation Proclamation" was made after the northern victory at the bloody battle of Antietam, and was to become law on the first day of 1863.

The slave owners were not impressed. Lincoln was the president of a foreign country, they said, so he had no right to make proclamations about the Confederacy—the slaves were still slaves. But the move encouraged more slaves to join the Union army.

In 1865, after four years of desperate fighting and hundreds of thousands of deaths, the South surrendered. The United States was "united" once more, whether the South liked it or not. That same year, a brief amendment was added to the American Constitution:

Neither slavery nor involuntary servitude, except as a punishment for crime whereof the party shall have been duly convicted, shall exist within the United States, or any place subject to their jurisdiction.

With those simple words, the long years of American slavery were over.

In 1865 the Confederate army surrendered, and the president of the Confederacy was captured and put in prison. After four years of terrible bloodshed and destruction, the war was over. Some thirty-eight thousand black soldiers had died in the fight to abolish slavery, but those who survived went home to their families with the knowledge that they were free — and free forever.

The Underground Railroad was no longer needed. The black people of the United States were finally free.

THE DESTRUCTION OF THE SOUTH
By the end of the war, the cities and plantations of the South lay in ruins.

The Union armies had destroyed the homes and cities they passed through, looting and vandalizing as they went. The death toll had been appalling. The great mansions were crumbling, the grand families were bankrupt, the fields were barren and empty. The slave owners had clung to slavery because their way of life depended on it—and now it was gone.

The first black regiment in the war, the Fifty-fourth Massachusetts Volunteers, attacks Fort Wagner, South Carolina, in July 1863. Many whites had predicted that blacks would make poor soldiers, but this battle proved their courage. One sergeant won the Congressional Medal of Honor for his outstanding bravery in the action.

The battle for freedom was not quite over. Since they couldn't have slavery, the southern states tried to pass "black codes" to limit the rights of blacks, especially their right to own land and vote. But further amendments to the Constitution declared that states had no right to pass such laws, or to base voting rights on "race, color, or previous condition of servitude."

EXODUS FROM THE NORTH

During the Civil War, the Union had sent recruiting agents up to Canada to enlist black soldiers, and many had left their homes and families and gone to join the fighting. Among them was Harriet Tubman—"Moses"— who went to serve as a nurse to the thousands of slaves escaping to the Union army. She was also a scout and a spy, venturing into Confederacy

Anderson Ruffin Abbott was the first Canadian-born black doctor. His father, Wilson Ruffin Abbott, had been a free black shopkeeper in Alabama until antiblack legislation and ill treatment drove the family to Toronto in 1835; forty years later he owned more than seventy-five properties and was active in church, politics, and the Anti-Slavery Society. His son, Anderson, graduated from the University of Toronto in 1860 and served as a surgeon in the Union army during the Civil War, but returned to Canada after the war to become a prominent town leader.

Many blacks in Canada returned to the United States to take part in the war for freedom. Dr. Martin Delany had moved to Chatham in 1856, and had lectured and written about abolition as well as carrying on his medical practice. Delany believed North American blacks should create their own nation, and he went to Africa and bought land for that purpose. During the Civil War he was a major — the highest rank any black held in that war — and worked as a recruiter. After the war he moved back to the United States; his plan for an African settlement came to nothing.

territories to find warehouses and ammunition stores, and leading commando troops in to destroy them. After the war, Tubman moved back to the United States to live.

Alexander Ross, the white bird-watcher from Ontario who had secretly advised slaves on how to escape, also played a part in the war. President Lincoln knew that a Confederate spy ring was smuggling messages across the border, and asked Dr. Ross to investigate. Ross discovered that the ringleader was a woman, and led her into the hands of American detectives, who found eighty-two secret messages sewn into her underclothes.

After the war, many of the blacks who had fled to Canada returned to the United States. Of about forty thousand who had moved north, perhaps twenty-five thousand decided to go back. They no longer had to fear slavery, and now the United States could offer them the same legal protections that they had in Canada.

Even with those protections, they faced an enormous battle. Their years of slavery had left many blacks poor and uneducated. Some whites preferred to go on believing that they were naturally superior. Families ruined by the war often blamed the blacks, and hated them. Blacks would suffer many years of mean and unfair treatment, and sometimes violence, as they worked to overcome the long-lasting effects of slavery. Today, in the United States and in Canada, problems and prejudices still remain.

But while the story of slavery is an ugly one, it is finally a story of justice overcoming injustice. It's a story of wrongs being made right — not easily, not quickly, but through the determination of men and women, black and white. And through the gloom of the slave years we can imagine a network of shining silver tracks — tracks of persistence and kindness and unimaginable courage — as so many people made their way to freedom on the Underground Railroad.

Afterword

After the slaves in the United States were freed, slavery became less and less accepted among other nations. In 1890, representatives of eighteen countries met in Belgium to sign a treaty against the African slave trade. In 1926, the League of Nations adopted strong anti-slavery conventions. In 1948, the United Nations' Declaration of Human Rights banned slave-owning and slave-trading. Today no country in the world admits to allowing slavery.

And yet the practice goes on, under different disguises. In some countries, small children are sold into "adoption" and then used as household servants. Young women are "married" against their will, to whoever pays the best "bride price," while young men are acquired as "pupils"—both end up doing heavy labor. Tenant farmers are charged so much "rent" for their land that they are hopelessly in debt; since they aren't allowed to move until they pay off this debt, they are captive for life. In too many countries, people who are poor and uneducated can still find themselves in a life that is simply slavery by another name.

All the same, the days of slave-owning are numbered. As democracy continues its spread around the world, slavery is recognized as a shameful practice. Space-age communications carry modern ideas and modern hopes to oppressed people in far corners of the globe, and expose the oppressors—and their governments—to international censure. For those who would live by enslaving others, there is no place left to hide.

"It is the wickedest thing a man can do to hold a slave—the most unconscionable sin a man can do."
Isaac Williams, ex-slave

"My idea of slavery is, that it is one of the blackest, the wickedest things that ever were in the world."
Nancy Howard, ex-slave

"I look at slavery as the most horrid thing on earth."
William Henry Bradley, ex-slave

⟞⟝

"If slavery is not wrong, nothing is wrong."
Abraham Lincoln

Chronology

1400s	Portuguese sailors begin shipping Africans to Europe to be slaves.
Early 1500s	First slave ships from Africa arrive in the New World (in the mainly Spanish and Portuguese colonies of South and Central America).
1600s	Slave trade is expanded to North America, to supply the British and French colonies of New England and New France.
1619	First African slaves reach Virginia.
1628	First record of a slave arriving directly from Africa to New France.
1689	Louis XIV, the French king, gives French colonists permission to keep slaves, a practice forbidden in France itself.
1760	British conquer New France. As part of the war settlement, the British agree that the status of slaves will not be changed.
1772	Slaves in England are given their freedom, although it is still legal for the English to take part in the international slave trade.
1775	American Revolution begins when the thirteen American colonies rise up against Britain. The British promise freedom to any American slaves who fight on the English side. Loyalists move to Canada with their slaves.
1787	American Constitution declares that slaves who escape to a free state must be returned to their masters.
1793	First Fugitive Slave Act is passed by the U.S. Congress, making it a crime for anyone in the United States to help runaway slaves or prevent their arrest. The Lieutenant-Governor of Upper Canada, John Graves Simcoe, passes an act saying that any slave who reaches Upper Canada will become free.
Early 1800s	Underground Railroad is first organized.
1807	British Parliament bans all trading and shipping of African slaves. The United States makes it illegal to bring more slaves in from outside the country, although slaves can still be traded within the slave-owning states.

1812   The War of 1812 breaks out when the United States declares war on Britain and attacks Canada. Again, the British offer land and freedom to American blacks who fight on their side.

1819   Canadians deny the American government's request for cooperation in returning slaves who escaped to Canada, and for permission to pursue escaped slaves into Canadian territory.

1820   Under the Missouri Compromise, Missouri enters the Union as a slave-holding state and Maine enters as a free state, keeping the number of free and slaveholding states even.

1826   Canada formally refuses to return runaway slaves to the United States.

1833   British Parliament passes the Abolition Act, abolishing slavery throughout the British Empire.

1850   The Compromise of 1850 attempts to resolve a furious debate over whether slavery should be allowed in Texas, California, Utah, and New Mexico. The passage of the second Fugitive Slave Act is part of the compromise.

1852   *Uncle Tom's Cabin* by Harriet Beecher Stowe is published.

1859   A group of black and white abolitionists, led by John Brown, raid a government arsenal at Harpers Ferry, Virginia, for guns and ammunition to raid surrounding plantations and free slaves. John Brown is hanged for treason, conspiracy, and murder.

1860   Abraham Lincoln, leader of the Republican Party, is elected president of the United States. Seven of the southern states break away from the Union to form their own country.

1861   Confederate forces attack Fort Sumter in South Carolina and the American Civil War begins.

1862   President Lincoln issues the Emancipation Proclamation, abolishing slavery in the rebel southern states as of January 1, 1863.

1865   The South surrenders to the North and the slaves are freed. Lincoln is fatally shot by John Wilkes Booth. An amendment is added to the American Constitution outlawing slavery.

Source Notes

(Publisher and date are given where a book is first referred to, unless the book is included in the Suggested Reading or Selected Bibliography.)

Chapter 2

Equiano quotation is from Olaudah Equiano, *The Slave Who Bought His Freedom*, ed. K. Kennedy (New York: Dutton, 1971), cited in Richard Howard, *Black Cargo*.

Austin Bearse quotation is from Austin Bearse, *Reminiscences of Fugitive Slave Law Days* (Boston: Warren Richardson, 1880), cited in Charles L. Blockson, *The Underground Railroad*.

Chapter 3

Douglass quotation is cited in *Black Cargo*.

Henson quotation is from Josiah Henson, *The Life of Josiah Henson*.

CAPTIONS

Governor of French West Indies quotation is cited in *Black Cargo*.

John Brown quotation is cited in Jim Haskins, *Get on Board*.

Chapter 4

CAPTIONS

Quotation re woman in woods is from Octavia V. Rogers Albert, *The House of Bondage* (New York, 1891), cited in Dorothy Sterling, ed., *We Are Your Sisters*.

Chapter 5

Henderson and Younger quotations are from Benjamin Drew, *A North-Side View of Slavery* (Boston: J. P. Jewett & Co., 1856), cited in Blockson, *The Underground*

Railroad. (Non-quotations from John Jackson and anonymous woman from Mississippi are from the same source.)

Evans and Taylor quotations are from William Troy, *Hairbreadth Escapes from Slavery to Freedom.*

CAPTIONS

Warren quotation is cited in Benjamin Drew, *The Refugee.*

Chapter 6

Quotation from Charley is from Eber M. Pettit, *Sketches in the History of the Underground Railroad* (Fredonia, N.Y.: McKinstry & Son, 1879), cited in Blockson, *The Underground Railroad.*

Fisher quotation is from Horatio T. Struther, *The Underground Railroad in Connecticut* (Middletown, Connecticut: Wesleyan University Press, 1962), cited in Blockson, *The Underground Railroad.*

Gragston quotation is from "The Bell and the Light," in B. A. Botkin, ed., *Lay My Burden Down.*

Chapter 7

Tubman quotation "I think slavery" is cited in *The Refugee.*

Tubman quotation "I had reasoned" is cited in *Get on Board.*

Garrett quotations are from *Get on Board* and Blockson, *The Underground Railroad.*

Fairbanks quotation is from Reverend Calvin Fairbanks, "During Slavery Times," in Wilbur H. Siebert, *The Underground Railroad from Slavery to Freedom* (London: Macmillan, 1898), cited in Daniel G. Hill, *The Freedom-Seekers.*

Chapter 8

The two Whittier quotations are from "Our Countrymen in Chains" and "The New Year," from John Greenleaf Whittier, *The Complete Poetical Works of Whittier* (Boston: Houghton Mifflin, 1894).

Garrison quotation is cited in *Get on Board.*

Loguen and Parker quotations are cited in Blockson, *The Underground Railroad.*

Patrick Snead quotation is cited in *The Refugee.*

Quotation about Patty Cannon is from Charles L. Blockson, "Escape from Slavery: The
    Underground Railroad," *National Geographic*, vol.166, no.1, July 1984.
Toronto Patriot quotation and Leonard quotation are cited in *The Freedom-Seekers*.
CAPTIONS
Douglass quotation is cited in Empak Publishing, "A Salute to Historic Black
    Americans."
Truth quotation is cited in *We Are Your Sisters*.

Chapter 9

White quotation is from "Where Lincoln Wrote His Name," in *Lay My Burden
    Down*.
Lincoln quotation is cited in Stuart Berg Flexner, *I Hear America Talking: An Illustrated
    History of American Words and Phrases* (New York: Simon and Schuster, 1979).
All other quotations are from Harriet Beecher Stowe, *Uncle Tom's Cabin*.
CAPTIONS
Stowe quotation about herself is cited in *Get on Board*.
Quotation about "Eliza" is from *Uncle Tom's Cabin*.
Brown quotation is cited in *Get on Board*.

Chapter 10

Williamson quotation is from *The Refugee*.
Sinclair and McCullum quotations are from S. G. Howe, *The Refugees from Slavery*.
Miller quotation is from *The Refugee*.
Sunter letter is from *The Brantford Expositor*, June 10, 1859, cited in *The Freedom-Seekers*.
Brown and Simpson quotations are from *The Refugees from Slavery*.
Grose quotation is from *The Refugee*.
Henson quotations are from *The Life of Josiah Henson*.
Quotation about Toronto blacks is from *The Freedom-Seekers*. George Brown quotation is
    from *The Refugees from Slavery*.
CAPTIONS
Williamson quotation is from *The Refugee*.
Victoria Pioneer Rifles quotation is from Kilian, *Go Do Some Great Thing*.

Chapter 11

Quotations are from the Constitution of the United States, Amendment XIII, Section
I, and Amendment XV, Section I.

CAPTIONS

Lincoln quotation is cited in Lord Longford, *Abraham Lincoln*.

Afterword

Williams, Howard, and Bradley are cited in *The Refugee*.

Lincoln's remark is from a letter to A. G. Hodges, April 4, 1864, cited in *The Home Book
of Quotations*, by Burton Stevenson (New York: Dodd Mead, 1967).

Suggested Reading

Blockson, Charles L. *The Underground Railroad*. New York: Prentice Hall, 1987.

Botkin, B. A., ed. *Lay My Burden Down: A Folk History of Slavery*. New York: Dell, 1994.

Bramble, Linda. *Black Fugitive Slaves in Early Canada*. St. Catharines: Vanwell, 1988.

Haskins, Jim. *Get on Board: The Story of the Underground Railroad*. New York: Scholastic, 1993.

Henson, Josiah. *The Life of Josiah Henson, Formerly a Slave*. Boston: Arthur D. Phelps, 1849. Republished by Dresden, Ontario: Uncle Tom's Cabin Museum, 1965.

Hill, Daniel G. *The Freedom-Seekers: Blacks in Early Canada*. Agincourt, Ontario: Book Society of Canada, 1981.

Howard, Richard. *Black Cargo*. London: Wayland, 1972.

Lind, Jane. *The Underground Railroad: Anna Maria Weems*. Toronto: Grolier, 1990.

Longford, Lord. *Abraham Lincoln*. London: Weidenfeld and Nicolson, 1974.

Pinney, Roy. *Slavery Past and Present*. Don Mills, Ontario: Nelson, 1972.

Stowe, Harriet Beecher. *Uncle Tom's Cabin, or Life among the Lowly/The Minister's Wooing/Oldtown Folks*. New York: Literary Classics of the United States, 1982.

Selected Bibliography

Bertley, Leo W. *Canada and Its People of African Descent*. Pierrefonds, Quebec: Bilongo Publishers, 1977.

Drew, Benjamin. *The Refugee: or The Narratives of Fugitive Slaves in Canada*. Boston: John P. Jewett, 1856.

Empak Publishing. *A Salute to Historic Black Abolitionists*. Chicago: Empak Publishing, 1988.

Howe, S. G. *The Refugees from Slavery in Canada West: Report to the Freedmen's Inquiry Commission*. Boston: Wright & Potter, 1864.

Hughes, Langston, and Milton Meltzer. *A Pictorial History of the Negro in America*. New York: Crown, 1956.

Kilian, Crawford. *Go Do Some Great Thing: The Black Pioneers of British Columbia*. Vancouver: Douglas & McIntyre, 1978.

Pachai, Bridglal. *Blacks*. Tantalon, N.S.: Four East, 1987.

Soderlund, Jean R. *Quakers & Slavery: A Divided Spirit*. Princeton, N.J.: Princeton University Press, 1987.

Sterling, Dorothy, ed. *We Are Your Sisters: Black Women in the Nineteenth Century*. Markham, Ontario: Penguin, 1984.

Troy, William. *Hairbreadth Escapes from Slavery to Freedom*. Manchester, England: W. Bremner, 1861.

Walker, James W. St. G. *The Black Loyalists: The Search for a Promised Land in Nova Scotia and Sierra Leone 1783-1870*. New York: Africana, 1976.

Acknowledgments

Thanks to Malcolm Lester and Kathy Lowinger at Lester Publishing, who proposed this project and entrusted it to me; also to Beverley Endersby, the editor's editor. For research assistance I am indebted to Barbara Hehner; Everette Moore, Aileen Williams, and Marion Byard at the Ontario Black History Society in Toronto; Alice Newby and Charlene Freeman at the Raleigh Township Centennial Museum in North Buxton, Ontario; Elise Harding-Davis at the North American Black Historical Museum in Amherstburg, Ontario; Patrice Chapman and Margaret Ward at the Museum of African American History in Detroit; Jane Sweet at the Society of Friends in Toronto and Jane Zavitz-Bond at Pickering (Quaker) College; Pierre-Louis Lapointe of the Archives Nationales du Québec; staff of the Metropolitan Toronto Reference Library and the Ontario Archives; and many other patient and knowledgeable archivists, too numerous to mention.

G.K.G.

Picture Sources

⊰⊱⇒ ⇐⊰⊱

Every reasonable effort has been made to trace the ownership of copyright materials. Any information allowing the publisher to correct a reference or credit in future will be welcomed.

For space reasons the following abbreviations have been used:

LOC: Library of Congress (Washington)

MC: Mansell Collection Limited (London)

MEPL: Mary Evans Picture Library (London)

NABHM: North American Black Historical Museum, Inc.
            (Amherstburg, Ontario)

NAC: National Archives of Canada

MTRL: Metropolitan Toronto Reference Library

NYHS: New York Historical Society

OBHS: Ontario Black History Society (Toronto)

Facing p. 1 MTRL; p. 3 *Pollice Verso* (oil on canvas, c. 1859) by Jean-Léon Gérôme, Phoenix Art Museum, 68.52; p. 4-5 MC; p. 6 MEPL; p. 9 MC; p. 10 National Maritime Museum, D4695 (Greenwich, England); p. 13 MEPL; p.15 NABHM; p. 16 MC; p. 19 Louisiana State Museum, 1990:49; p. 20 MC; p. 22 OBHS; p. 25 *Gazette de Québec*, Archives Nationales du Québec; p. 26 Missouri Historical Society, Groups/263; p. 28 NAC, PAC-252; p. 31 Schomburg Center for Research in Black Culture, New York Public Library, SC-CN-92-0052; p. 34 *The Promise*, by J. Walter West, Society of Friends, Toronto; p. 39, 40, 43 MC; p. 47 Terence Dickinson; p. 49 Brooklyn Museum, 40.58.A; p. 50 OBHS; p.54 *Fugitive Slaves in the Dismal Swamp* (oil on canvas, 1888) by David Cronin, NYHS #1914.11; p. 58 Photograph Collection, Public Archives of Nova Scotia; p. 61 NYHS #61659; p. 62 MC; p. 65 National Film Board, courtesy OBHS; p. 68 "Southern Ideas of Liberty," courtesy, American Antiquarian Society (Worcester,

Mass.), 01609; p.71 LOC, LC-USZ62-1286; p. 77 Lenawee County Historical Society (Adrian, Michigan); p. 78 MTRL; p. 80 Schomburg Center for Research in Black Culture, New York Public Library, SC-CN-91-0139/92-0715; p. 83, 85 OBHS; p. 88 MTRL #963 C2/2; p. 91 National Portrait Gallery, Smithsonian Institution, NPG.74.75; p. 93 MC; p. 96 National Film Board, courtesy OBHS; p. 98 Schomburg Center for Research in Black Culture, New York Public Library, SC-CN-90-0379; p.104 Berenice Lowe Collection, Bentley Historical Library, University of Michigan; p. 107 NYHS #41090; p. 108 NYHS #38219; p. 109 LOC, LC-USZ62-30828; p. 110 NYHS #33236; p. 111 courtesy Barbara Carter at Uncle Tom's Cabin Historical Site, Dresden, Ontario; p. 112 *The Underground Railroad*, by Charles T. Webber, Cincinnati Art Museum #1927.26; p. 117 MC; p. 121 NAC, PAC-123708; p. 125 OBHS; p.128 *The Freedom-Seekers* (book), by Daniel G. Hill; p. 131 OBHS; p. 132 top MTRL #355.12 W38; p. 132 bottom NABHM; p. 133 top British Columbia Archives and Records Service #4967 A-2015; p. 133 bottom NABHM; p. 134 MTRL #963 C2/31; p. 135 NAC, PAC-C29977; p. 136-37 Raleigh Township Centennial Museum, North Buxton, Ontario; p.138 British Columbia Archives and Records Service #53094 C-6124; p. 141 NAC, PAC-C7041; p.143 *The Slave Trade* (book), by Anne Mountfield; p. 144 LOC, LC-USZ62-5334; p.146 LOC, LC-USZ62-175; p. 147 LOC, LC-USZ62-1288; p. 148 MTRL, S-90 A. R. Abbott Papers; p. 149 OBHS.

Index